D1153584

Cooking and surfing
on the West Coast of Ireland

By **Jane** and **Myles Lamberth**
with **Shannon Denny**

THE SURF CAFÉ COOKBOOK
Cooking and surfing on the West Coast of Ireland

Jane and Myles Lamberth
With Shannon Denny

Published by Orca Publications

EDITOR: Louise Searle
COPY EDITOR: Shannon Denny
PHOTOGRAPHER: Mike Searle
DESIGNER: David Alcock
ASSISTANT DESIGNER: Alistair Marshall
ILLUSTRATIONS: Paula Mills, Emily Hamilton, David Alcock, Alistair Marshall
PRODUCTION: Chris Power

PHOTOGRAPHIC CONTRIBUTORS: Mark Capitallan, Aaron Pierce, Louise Searle, Mickey Smith, Roger Sharp, Jason Feast, Seahound, David Alcock

The Surf Café Cookbook ISBN 978-0-9567893-1-0

PRINTED AND BOUND: Great Wall Printing, Hong Kong
Published by Orca Publications
Berry Road Studios, Berry Road, Newquay, Cornwall, TR7 1AT, United Kingdom
TEL: (+44) 01637 878074 **FAX:** (+44) 01637 850226 **WEB:** www.orcasurf.co.uk

Copyright 2012 Orca Publications
All rights reserved. No part of this book may be reproduced, stored or transmitted in any form without written permission from the publisher. The publisher has tried to make the information in this book as accurate as possible and accepts no responsibility for any loss, injury or inconvenience sustained by any person using the book.

CONTENTS

WELCOME TO SHELLS CAFÉ!

Here we make fresh, innovative, tasty, unpretentious food right by the sea. We use fresh, organic, seasonal produce from the bounty of Irish soil and waters.

We love our community, which is a special one made up of surfers and people who love to be outside. A passion for great food and a great environment drives what we do. Shells is a hub of good food, good vibes, creativity and outdoor living.

We want to share this rich experience with you. Sláinte!

Jane & Myles

A LITTLE ABOUT SHELLS

Myles and I met over eight years ago when we were both working at the Headland Hotel in Newquay. When our paths first crossed, we had both had enough of city life and were taking time out in Cornwall to surf. We thought it was a summer fling, but it's definitely lasted longer than that! After the summer ended, we spent our winters running chalets in ski resorts and our summers working in restaurants by the sea. In between we guided safari trips through South Africa, Namibia, Zimbabwe and Mozambique. We made our life about our passions – food and the outdoors.

When Myles and I eventually felt the need to be somewhere for more than six months, we looked high and low for the right location. We visited Myles' family in New Zealand, Australia and South Africa to see if we could live in any of those places. We tried living in the French Alps, The Rockies and California, and we searched all over Ireland too – Lahinch, Cork and of course Sligo. We were were getting nowhere fast and just couldn't find the right place, until one day Shells came on the market.

The minute we saw it I knew it was for us. We harassed the landlord, Stephen Taylor, so much that he finally gave in and agreed to rent to us. We'd never lived in Sligo or Strandhill, but sometimes you just have to go with your instinct. We moved in and within 10 days we opened Shells for the first time on 31 March 2010.

We haven't looked back since. Strandhill is perfect for us and we love it. We're passionate about our little corner of this special place. During our travels we've seen what makes a good café and hopefully that comes across in what we do. We've taken elements from cafés in Melbourne, menu ideas from France and America, and coffee skills from Wellington in New Zealand, one of the leading coffee drinking cultures in the world.

Myles is head chef and mastermind behind the menu; his creative flair comes across in the presentation of the food and the mixing of flavours. We source most of our products locally, and support small Irish producers. This isn't marketing spin; we do it because the quality and freshness is amazing, and it makes our food better when we use the best ingredients. The recipes we've used have become favourites in the café. The meals we serve look just like the ones in the photos, they haven't had hours of food styling to make them look like that, what you see if what you get. No retouching here!

Sometimes running Shells seems too good to be true – I can hardly believe we have the privilege of living here and interacting with Strandhill's vibrant and endlessly creative community. In this book we not only want to share some of our food adventures, but also to celebrate this exceptionally beautiful part of Ireland and the incredible population that dwells in it.

So, welcome to our world – step right in and pull up a seat.

Coney Island

Pub

Strandhill beach

Shells Café

MARK CAPILITAN

RADKA

RADKA

MEET JANE...

Born: Dublin, Ireland

Loves: "People! I can talk all day, every day. I also love a good glass of white wine..."

Hates: "Traffic, having to queue and - if I'm honest - late nights."

Bio in a nutshell: Did a degree in business and marketing then worked for a large multinational company before ditching city life for a path of adventure; met Myles in Cornwall while working and surfing; spent five years travelling and working together across France, Africa, California and Ireland.

Jane

JANE & MYLES

MEET MYLES...

Born: Cape Town, South Africa

Loves: "Fresh air, the outdoors, adventure, being creative and food - ice cream is top of the list."

Hates: "Bureaucracy and Brussels sprouts."

Bio in a nutshell: Quit a fine arts course in order to become a river and safari guide; learned to cater for guests by cooking on riverside campfires; worked in the off-seasons as a chef around the world; ran chalets in France and America during ski seasons.

Myles

THE SURFING LIFE...

Myles on surfing:

"Luckily for me, I grew up on the beach in South Africa. My parents threw me into the pool when I was about three months old and I've been paddling ever since. Muizenberg is a great learners' wave, nice and soft, and I started there on a boogie board. At age 12 I sold my model trains and bought a surfboard and a really bad wetsuit. My uncle took me out and I stood up on my third wave. I just love the water, so I did water polo and free diving too. When we moved to Sligo, it was for the surf. When you're in the water you think of nothing else – it all washes away so you focus on the moment."

Jane on surfing:

"I love being in the sea and by the sea. I've always loved the culture of surfing so when it was coming on in Ireland a group of us went to Waterford for a lesson. Looking back, the conditions were atrocious! Onshore, one foot and mushy. But I just loved it – the escapism and all that it presented. I'm really into the carefree gracefulness of longboarding, and also the fact that it draws together like-minded people, music and art. The more I surf with Myles, the more it becomes ingrained in our life. It's a great way to switch off and stop thinking about the day. Being in the water and having a great surf can feel just like a holiday in itself; you can't beat the feeling."

in order to discover new lands
one has to lose sight of the shore

HOW TO MAKE FOOD TASTE GOOD

This book is full of recipes that can be used as building blocks. We aim to show you the basics but hope you'll feel inspired to add your own flair to each dish so that it reflects your taste. If you like what you've made then you're more likely to make it in the future. And for us that's a successful cookbook, one that you use again and again.

We also hope you will treat this book as a working project, so get stuck in and write notes so that the next time you approach a recipe you'll have your own tips there too. For example, every oven is different and cooking times may vary, so take notice of how your own cooker behaves and jot this down alongside the recipes.

Top tips

1) Read each recipe through before you start. There's nothing worse than not having an ingredient or missing a step. It's key to be prepared, so make sure you understand what you have to do in advance.

2) We always measure out dry goods first and have them ready and waiting. It makes the process a bit easier.

3) Don't be afraid to experiment and put your own style on the dish, but remember: while you can always add more flavour you can't take it away. With this in mind, use teaspoons and measuring cups instead of free pouring.

4) To keep in tune with current trends use cookbooks, food mags and cookery programmes for tips and inspiration. Even when you eat out, don't be afraid to ask what herbs or flavours are in a dish.

5) Fresh. Fresh. Fresh! There's great flavour and colour in fresh herbs.

This is one very easy – but profound – change you can make to your cooking.

6) Keep it seasonal and local. We sometimes feel that these words are thrown around like marketing tools, but the quality and flavour are so much better when foods are sourced locally. Adjust your fruit and veg choices to reflect the seasons.

7) Feel your food! Don't just pick up the first avocado on the shelf or the first garlic bulb you come across. Feel produce when shopping and look at the skin to choose the best ingredients available.

8) Good ingredients deliver good meals. Start using a butcher and deli, and ask for advice on products that meet your needs and your budget. These people are a huge source of knowledge. For example, a good butcher can often recommend a cheaper cut of meat

if you explain the meal you're trying to create.

9) Invest in one good knife. It will make your life so much easier. When buying, make sure you hold it first and that it's comfortable for you, because you're going to be the one using it. For pots and pans the general rule is the heavier the better.

10) Don't forget, you eat with your eyes too, so never send out a bland looking dish. We always use greenery in Shells, either with fresh herbs or flavoured oils. Add edible flowers to salads, or garnish with finely chopped bright veg, like radishes.

11) But our best advice is: have fun! Cook what you like to eat and don't get too worked up about the tasks ahead. Give yourself enough time to make the dish AND enough time to sit down and enjoy it afterwards.

TIP: Keep your kitchen knives razor sharp!

- Make sure only one person sharpens the knives, as different people use different angles.
- Sharp knives are really important, so keep on top of it.
- A sharpening steel is the best to use, but the technique takes a lot of practice. If you're really bad at it, take your knives to your local butcher and they'll no doubt be happy to oblige, and it will only take a few minutes too! (Make sure to buy some meat though, and that will ensure he'll do it again for you.) It's a really good way to start a nice relationship with your butcher.

THE PERFECT IRISH LARDER
Essential items for the kitchen

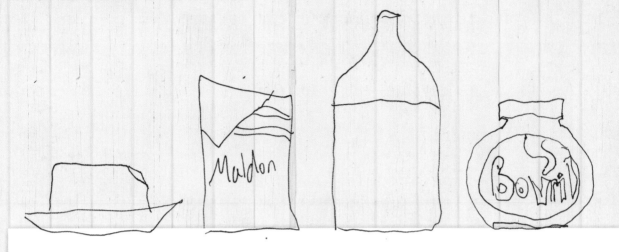

Butter
We use Connacht Gold. Butter in Ireland is great, with all the fat cows producing creamy milk.

Sea salt flakes
Better than ground salt and not as strong as rock salt. Crisp flakes of salt give a lovely seasoning to any dish.

Flavoured oils
Add a bit more depth to salads and stir-fries. Always have a basic vegetable oil, a good olive oil and rapeseed oil, which is made and grown in Ireland. Donegal raoeseed oil is a good one to try; it holds a higher temperature and the toasted oil lends interesting flavouring.

Dried herbs
Our most popular to use are cumin, coriander, curry, garam masala and fennel seed. I don't like to use green dried herbs as these are readily available fresh, so I tend to use fresh herbs where possible.

Bovril
For flavour!

Worcestershire sauce and soy sauce

Tabasco or peri-peri sauce
When spice is needed.

Red fruit jam
Not just for toast! This is always good for cooking with meats. Cranberry, loganberry or other jams add a nice sweetness to meat dishes.

Vinegars
White wine, good cider vinegar and balsamic; mix and match to make excellent dressings for salad leaves.

Dry sherry and brandy
Great for sautéing and adding to creamy sauces and gravies.

Fish sauce
A superb addition to Asian style dishes.

On the windowsill
Grow two pots of basil, coriander, rosemary and flat leaf parsley. Easy to keep and great to have on hand when cooking.

A range of flours
Some for baking, self-raising and strong flour for bread. Flour keeps very well, so it's worth having to hand.

Get to know your local suppliers. Ask them about what's good and what's in season. This will greatly improve your knowledge, and your meals. It will also enhance your shopping experience.

Essential kitchen implements

- Sharp knives
- Decent hand blender
- Kitchen Aid or food processor
- Good whisk
- Electronic scales (easier to use than analogue ones)
- Slotted spoon
- A good pan! Pay cheap, pay twice. The heavier the pan the better. Look for a good thick bottom and metal handles so you can cross from hob to oven.

HOW TO STOCK A
VEG BASKET

Beetroot

All beetroots aren't pink and purple; there are loads of different varieties and colours. We love to use these in salads with some creamy goats cheese and nuts – especially hazelnuts. Beetroot is also full of antioxidants, so a great option for a hangover! Beetroot Soup is a very well known cure. At Shells we grow golden and candied beetroot which has a white stripe in our little garden. We love to introduce guests to new varieties, and it's a bit of a talking point too!

HEALTHWISE: *Beetroot is an outstanding source of folic acid; it's also loaded with vitamin C, potassium, manganese and fibre.*

Celeriac

This is a probably the world's ugliest veg, but offers some of the world's greatest flavours and textures. It's so versatile you can do anything with it. Cook it, roast it, blend it or eat it raw. At Shells we use it in soups, coleslaw and an amazing remoulade (which is like a posh coleslaw), to go with our smoked salmon. To make the remoulade, grate celeriac with a nice homemade mustard mayonnaise. Add some freshly chopped dill at the end and give a light mix. This is great with salads, cold meats and fish.

HEALTHWISE: *Celeriac is good source of potassium, phosphorous, dietary fibre and vitamins B6 and C.*

Fennel

With its strong flavour, this can be eaten raw or roasted and is brilliant in soups. We do a lovely fennel and tomato soup in Shells, a nice alternative to the norm. Chop the fennel and sweat it down with onions before adding the tomatoes and – voilà – a new twist on tomato soup. Another great way to use fennel is to thinly slice it (use a mandolin if you have one) and marinate in lemon and rapeseed oil dressing. This makes a great side to fish.

"In the past it seemed that us Irish had a very traditional approach to food, but now things have exploded. Our menu items are so different and creative but the amazing thing is we are still using Irish produce, just in a new way."

HEALTHWISE: *Fennel will give you fibre, vitamin C, folic acid, niacin and potassium. Their seeds, and the tea made from them, is said to relieve indigestion.*

Parsnip

A sensational relation of the carrot. Have you tried mashed parsnip cakes, parsnip and apple soup, parsnip curry or honey roasted parsnip? The list is endless and the flavour is always great. This is a lovely sweet vegetable.

HEALTHWISE: *Parsnips are a terrific source of fibre, particularly the soluble kind, so this veg can help lower cholesterol and keep blood sugar levels on an even keel. They also contain folic acid.*

Rhubarb

Don't call it a fruit! Rhubarb is actually a vegetable. A real taste of the countryside, it grows anywhere and everywhere. A word of warning: the leaves are poisonous, but the stems are amazing! Delicious simply stewed with some sugar and topped with fresh whipped cream. Another way we like to use it is baked in a pie. Best in spring.

HEALTHWISE: *Rhubarb stalks are a rich source of vitamin C, dietary fibre and calcium.*

Wild Garlic

We love love love wild garlic! So delicate and visual, the flower is full of flavour and looks so pretty on salads or sitting nicely on soups just before serving. To use the stems, treat them like scallions or spring onions and use in mash potato for exceptional flavour. It works well in Asian cooking too. Late spring and early summer are the best times to find it thriving in shady wooded areas. We're lucky as is grows like mad in a friend's garden. They come to Shells with big handfuls of it, so we do a trade – coffee and cake for the wonderful wild garlic!

HEALTHWISE: *Like its domesticated cousin, wild garlic is said to help reduce cholesterol and blood pressure. The juices of its leaves have an antiseptic quality.*

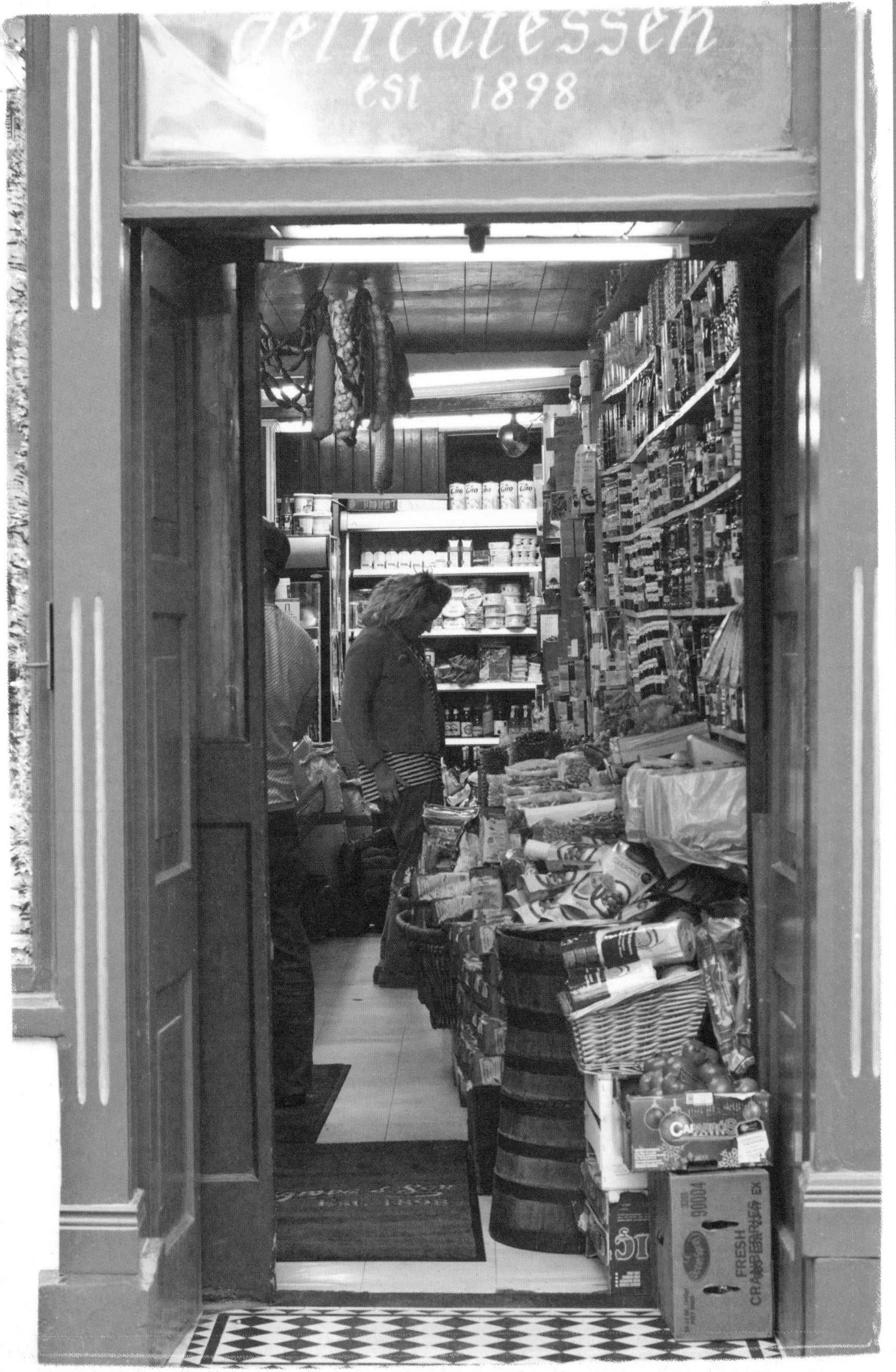
delicatessen
est 1898

WE ♡ DELIS

Delis are a treasure trove for foodies. Lots and lots of delightful jars, bottles and potions that inspire you to get back into the kitchen. I love that they are usually independently run and are full of goodies from your immediate area. I think it's really important to support these shops. It's the kind of shop that when it's gone you realise just how much you needed it. They always have those hard to find ingredients that will complete a recipe for a dinner party. For our Chai Lattes, we pick up small quantities of star anise. If we are making our own Turkish Delight we get little bottles of rose water to give them a lovely flavour and a beautiful hint of pink.

If they don't have what you are looking for they can usually get it in for you. I always speak to the owners, check what's just in and find out about any new products. I always say to friends, don't wait till the morning of your dinner party to get all the ingredients, ring ahead or pop in, it will be much easier for you in the long run.

To be honest our pet hate is trawling through a big shopping centre and a big super market. You end up filling your trolley with lots of items, cheap specials and the truth is, unless you are very disciplined most of it goes off before you even need it..... so although deli's appear a little more expensive, I think you actually think about what you put in your basket and you know what you are buying. To me a good deli is like a good bookshop. You enjoy taking the time to browse the shelves, stacked full of jars, bursting over with different products

Deli's are a great place to source local produce, the best salad leaves I get (apart from our garden) come directly from our local deli. Everything from cheese to chutney is generally made within the community. A major benefit of that is the money you spend stays in the community and sort of does a circle's that keeps everyone going.

Top 10 deli finds/ things to look for:

- good oils (if you haven't already made them from the book)
- speciality cheeses
- smoked meats
- quality salads, from hummus to coleslaw
- good olives and tapas style delights
- excellent range of herbal teas
- hard to find spices
- some will have great Irish chocolate/ artisan chocolate
- local honey
- fine wines (in most)

... AND COUNTRY MARKETS!

Irish Country Markets started way back in 1947. The organisation was set up to help local people maximise their resources and to keep money within the local community. Since then, it's grown and grown; there are now 62 markets around the country. A few years ago the Beltra Country Market opened down the road from Strandhill, and we absolutely love to go along on a Saturday to browse and buy.

A country market operates as a cooperative. Each seller pays an annual membership fee to join and is only allowed to sell the things they've grown, produced or made themselves. No one has an individual stall and sellers don't even have to stay while the market is in progress. Instead they can check their stuff in at the start, and then the organisers work out who has sold what at the end. That way, everyone can earn a little money.

With more awareness of food miles, provenance, processing and preservatives, there's an increasing consciousness about what goes into the food we eat. Meanwhile, interest is growing throughout the country in going back to basics as people get into in home baking, gardening and simple pleasures. Beltra Country Market is a lovely feature of the community and it's great to have this friendly local resource on our doorstep. We positively depend on it for fresh homegrown produce for the café too!

"Being Irish, supper was always the most important part of the day. We'd all sit around the table and chat about the day. (You know how we Irish like to chat!) Years ago very little was imported; everything was seasonal and grown around the corner. We've come full circle again. Our farmers and producers have adapted to new palates and demands and have started producing amazing food previously only available from abroad. We are even making our own Irish mozzarella! There's no need to not support Irish and I love that. Grow, nurture, produce and eat - all from Irish soil!"

TODAY'S SPECIAL

BREA...

- Irish Organic Porridge w...
- Irish Fruity Toast w homem...
- Skells Homemade Beans on...
- The Full House: Woodville... Sausage, g...
- Eggs Benedict: 2 Poached... Hollandaise...
- Bacon Sandwich w red s...
- Radka's Homemade Scon...
- Daily Breakfast Spec...

easy does it...

MICKEY SMITH

DAWN PATROL

The early bird catches the worm...

POWER SNACKS

One thing as a surfer you notice is some food gives you an immediate high and then boom – you crash. Processed foods that are full of refined carbohydrates make your blood sugar soar and then crash, which means you start craving them again. We've started to make as much food as we can ourselves and take control of what we're putting into our bodies...

You want something wholesome to see you through the day, to give you that energy to have a surf at first light or to keep you going to the top of that mountain. The type of food you need is food that will release energy slowly and sustain you.

Most of these snacks can be stored for up to a week in airtight containers, so you can make batches in advance and keep them in your glove box. That way if you check the surf and it's firing, grab a bite and hit it!

Local Honey Surf Energy Bars

Bake a batch and keep them in an airtight biscuit tin and they will last up to a week. Packed with energy, these are perfect for dawn patrol. You'll be ripping it up in the surf... Great to munch on after a surf too.

Makes 16

125g (½ cup) unsalted butter
150g (¾ cup) soft brown sugar or light muscovado sugar
75g (3½ tsp) honey, plus a little more to finish (we use Knocknarae honey, the best in the west!)
300g (3½ cups) porridge oats (not jumbo); at shells we use a local porridge called Kilbeggan
150g (1 cup) dried fruit (such as raisins, sultanas and chopped apricots, prunes or dates)
Handful of mixed seeds
Handful of whole nuts, eg hazelnuts, almonds, walnuts or pistachios

TIP: Whole nuts are often cheaper in Asian specialist food shops rather than the supermarket

METHOD

▪ Grease and line a baking tin, about 20cm/8" square. Put the butter, sugar and honey in a deep saucepan over a very low heat. Leave until melted, stirring from time to time.
▪ Stir the oats, dried fruit and whole nuts into the melted butter mixture. You're looking for a nice sticky consistency. Spread the mixture out evenly in the baking tin, smoothing the top as you go.
▪ Scatter seeds over the surface and trickle with a little more honey. Place in an oven preheated to 160°C/320°F/Gas Mark 3 and bake for about 30 minutes, until golden in the centre and golden brown at the edges.
▪ Leave to cool completely in the tin. Be patient – it cuts much better when cold. Then turn out and cut into squares with a sharp knife. These bars will keep for five to seven days in an airtight tin.

GOOD FOR ENERGY

Smoothies

Smoothies are quick and easy to make. They're so good for you and perfect pre- or post-surf.

Pear, Apple and Ginger Smoothie

Place two peeled, cored and roughly chopped pears and a half teaspoon of finely grated root ginger in a blender. Pour in 200ml (¾ cup) of apple juice and 50ml (¼ cup) of thick organic natural yogurt. Blitz until smooth and pour into glasses and serve. This is a great smoothie after a surf, as the ginger warms you inside and gets the circulation going again after the cold water.

Banana, Honey and Milk Smoothie

Place two peeled bananas, two tablespoons of honey and 300ml (1¼ cups) of milk in a blender. For a super thick smoothie mix you can throw in a spoon of malt too! Whiz until smooth. Pour into a glass to serve, stick a straw in and drink immediately. For a nice addition add a few drops of vanilla essence to this... delish! This is perfect pre-surf; with all the energy in this smoothie you're guaranteed a two-hour session with no hunger pangs!

Cranberry Flapjacks

Wonderfully moist and oaty. Flapjacks are perfect start to any day.

Makes 16

225g (2 cups) dried cranberries
55g (3 tbsp) golden syrup
170g (¾ cup) butter
100g (½ cup) caster sugar
250g (3 cups) rolled oats

Method

- Heat oven to 170°C/340°F and butter a 20 x 20cm baking dish.
- Put the cranberries in a bowl and cover with boiling water for a few minutes to rehydrate them. Drain away water and chop any large ones. They shouldn't be too big but leave them chunky enough that you can see them throughout the bar.
- Melt the syrup, butter and sugar together in a large pan over a gentle heat until the sugar has dissolved, then stir in the oats. Add most of the cranberries and stir through.
- Spoon the flapjack mixture into the tin and smooth it down with a spatula. Sprinkle the remaining cranberries on top.
- Bake in the oven for 30 to 35 minutes until golden. Mark the squares while still warm but only remove from the tin once cool. Also only cut once cold, as it will be much easier then.
- Enjoy with a big pot of chai tea!

MICKEY SMITH

AARON PIERCE

Your Homemade Granola

It is really worth making your own granola. The whole point is that you don't have to follow a strict recipe, you just add the nuts and seeds that you like. Mix and match different flavours and textures to suit your taste. Then serve it up with a big dollop of thick yoghurt and a drizzle of local honey.

You'll need a small pot, a big oven tray and a large wooden spoon.

Base ingredients:

500g (6¼ cups) rolled oats

150g (¾ cup) sunflower oil or vegetable oil

150ml (⅔ cup) of honey

100ml (½ cup) water

100g (½ cup) desiccated coconut

500g (4⅓ cups) seeds and nuts (Your choice, eg a handful of chopped nuts, hazelnuts, crushed pecans, almonds, sunflower seeds, pumpkin seeds, macadamia. A handful is around 75g (⅔ cup), so go mad and enjoy the mix.)

350g (2¾ cups) dried fruit mix, like chopped apricots, banana flakes, raisins, sultanas, dried blueberries, cranberries or cherries.

- Preheat oven to 180°C/350°F.
- In a small pot melt the oil and honey together.
- Stir in the water and bring to a gentle boil.
- In a separate large bowl mix the oats, coconut and nuts (save the dried fruits for later), and spread evenly into one or two oven trays. **TIP:** It's best to go for shallow, even roasting trays.
- Pour the warm liquid into the trays and stir together to obtain an even coating.
- Bake for 35 to 45 minutes, stirring every eight minutes or so for an even golden colour.
- Remove from the oven and leave to cool completely (while enjoying the amazing baking smells!) **TIP:** Stirring it up helps the cooling process.
- When cooled, stir in the dried fruit mix and pour into an airtight container – this is really important. If it's not airtight then your creation will go stale.

This will keep up to three months. Perfect for those early morning surf runs up and down the coast, searching for the right wave. On your way home stop into a shop and buy a thick organic yoghurt and just add your very own granola! You'll be ready for surf number two in no time…

Irish Porridge Three Ways

Serves 2

1 cup of Irish organic porridge oats
2 cups of milk or water
Splash of cream (optional)

"Top of the morning to ya!" Did you know the correct answer back is "And the rest of the day to yourself"?

There's no better way to start the day than a steamy bowl of good ol' porridge. At Shells we use Kilbeggan Organic Porridge from a family-run farm that goes back five generations. We've got three simple ways to spruce it up, but first the basics:

Method

- Place oats into a small pot on a medium heat.
- Pour in liquid and stir regularly for six to eight minutes. The porridge should be 'blupping away' blip blap, reducing the amount of liquid
- Add more milk or water as you cook to get the right consistency for you. I personally prefer a runny porridge.
- **TIP:** You're looking for a nice creamy consistency, not too thick. For an extra indulgence add a splash of cream.
- **TIP:** Stir, stir, stir! Don't take your eyes off it for too long.
- Allow to rest for one minute and then pour into two bowls.

Health tip: Oats are a great source of slow release energy... the perfect start for a two-surf day.

Now for the additions...

- Homemade fruit compote (see page 120), because there's nothing better than foraging berries in the summer and making a nice jam.
- Fried banana, toasted almonds (put flaked almonds in the oven for 10 minutes at 180°C/350°F – dry, no oil needed) and a drizzle of local honey. Sweet as!
- Toasted hazelnuts (same process as the almonds, but hazelnuts take a little longer, say 15 to 20 minutes, then rub the skins off with a kitchen towel), orange zest and a generous pour of Irish Mist (a sweet Irish liqueur to warm you up). A local alternative to hazelnuts are cobnuts, which are indigenous to Ireland. Something to look out for when foraging!
- Keep your porridge seasonal. So in the deepest winter, surprise your friends with a Christmas porridge fest! Add allspice and poached pears to your cooked porridge.
- Green porridge for Paddy's day, using grated green apples and pistachio for flavour and colour.

Cup of Chai!

Chai tea is a rich and complex beverage that's been savoured for centuries in many parts of the world, especially India. We serve up a homemade sweet version in Shells and it's such a hit! The sweetness takes a sip or two to get used to, but this is the traditional way to serve it. It's a great drink to warm you up after a surf or a hike and the spices give a lovely warm cosy feeling too!

In its most basic form, chai is black tea that's brewed strong with a combination of spices and diluted with milk and sugar.

The spices vary from recipe to recipe, but usually consist of cinnamon, cardamom, cloves, pepper, ginger and star anise. Chai tea is traditionally consumed hot and sweet. The sweetness is needed to bring out the full flavours of the spices.

Here's a simple recipe to make chai at home. This is what you'll need:

1½ cups water

1½ inch stick of cinnamon

8 cardamom pods

8 whole cloves

¼ inch fresh ginger root, sliced thin

2 or 3 cups milk

6 teaspoons sugar

3 teaspoons Darjeeling tea leaves

1 star anise

Method

- Place water, cinnamon, cardamom, cloves, star anise and ginger in a pot and bring to a boil.
- Cover and lower heat to low setting and simmer for 10 minutes.
- Add milk and sugar and again bring to simmer.
- Next, add the tea leaves, remove from heat and cover.
- Let steep for three minutes and strain. Enjoy!

WHERE TO SURF

The surfy atmosphere of Strandhill was a major draw for us, and we'd be lost without the surrounding coastline and its countless breaks. Shortboard or longboard? To rip or to trim? Paddle out or tow in? Here in the west of Ireland the world really is your oyster. While hidden reefs await the adventurous explorer, this is our list of the best-known breaks in the area.

JASON FEAST

Easkey
Within 1.5km of here you'll find about five limestone reef breaks, all fairly hectic, critical and quite busy. You really have know how to surf in order to charge Easkey.

STRANDHILL

EASKEY

ENNISCRONE

SEAHOUND

Enniscrone
Massive beach stretching 4km along a flat, sandy seabed. A magnet for beginners and a superb place to learn. Experts meanwhile can try Enniscrone Point, a fickle right-hand point break that's often described as the Jeffrey's Bay of Ireland.

Bundoran, The Peak

Frequent host to European and international comps. The v-shaped rock reef here produces what many consider to be one of the best waves in Europe. Not a spot for beginners.

BUNDORAN

MULLAGHMORE

SHARPY

AARON PIERCE

Mullaghmore

The opposite end of the spectrum. This big wave spot attracts international pros keen to ride 60-foot mountains of pitching seawater. Geographically, the set-up provides an exceptional viewing gallery where the spectator sits almost eye level with riders poised at the top of their huge waves produced by the reef below.

MARK CAPILITAN

Strandhill

West facing beach open to every direction of swell that the Atlantic offers. Consistent. Beginners and advanced surfers mix well here; it's forgiving for the former, but provides some great punchy little banks for the latter too. Great views and a very friendly vibe await in the water.

OUR LITTLE VILLAGE BY THE SEA. STRANDHILL.

MARK CAPUTAN

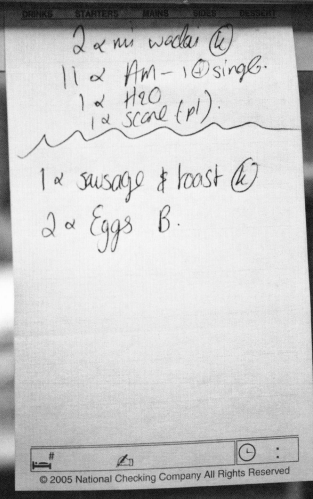

EASY
DOES IT

Breakfast like a king, lunch like a prince

and dinner like a pauper...

Poached Plums
with Toasted Almonds and Homemade Yoghurt

There's nothing worse than buying a big punnet of plums from the supermarket then getting home to find out they are tasteless and hard. But don't throw them away – we have a great plan for them. You can also use peaches or nectarines.

1 punnet of plums (about 8 large)
300g (1½ cups) caster sugar
250ml (1 cup) water
50g (½ cup) toasted flaked almonds, for garnish
200ml (¾ cup) homemade yoghurt or thick organic greek yoghurt
NOTE: If you only have small plums, reduce the sugar and water quantity.

Method:
- Cut the plums in half and remove the stones.
- On a low simmering heat, place the plums, sugar and water into a pot.
- Bring to a gentle boil for about 10 minutes until the plums are soft and the sweet syrup has turned a nice rosy red colour. Keep an eye on cooking time to avoid mushy plums.
- Give a light stir on occasion.
- Allow to cool and serve with yoghurt and toasted almonds.
TIP: There will be lots of lovely syrup left over, which is a delicious pink colour. Use in smoothies, over ice cream or add to sparkling water for a light refreshing drink!

Easy Homemade Yoghurt

1.5 litres (6⅛ cups) full cream milk
2 tablespoons fresh, organic, natural probiotic yoghurt (live!)

Method:
- Heat the milk in a heavy stainless steel saucepan to just under boiling point. Do not allow to boil, the temperature should be 85°C/ 185°F.
- Remove from the heat and allow to cool for 15 minutes or so. A perfect temperature would be between 39°C/100°F and 42°C/108°F.
- At this point stir in the live yoghurt and transfer to a glass bowl.
- Wrap the entire bowl with a tea towel and place in a nice warm area, eg next to the oven or close to a radiator. After five hours it should start to coagulate. Best to leave it overnight.
- The longer the mixture is kept warm, the better the flavour.
- When the yoghurt is set, transfer to the fridge and use as required.
- At this point you can add your favourite flavours, eg fruit compote or vanilla seeds.

TIP: Make the yoghurt the night before as it needs to set overnight.

TIP: To bake the flaked almonds, place on an oven tray in the oven at 180°C /350°F for 10 minutes. You do not need to add any oil or water. This dish works just as well with non toasted flaked almonds, but I personally prefer a bit more crunch from toasted almonds.

ALL HAPPINESS DEPENDS ON A LEISURELY BREAKFAST.
JOHN GUNTHER

Irish Potato Cakes

Makes 8

250g (1¼ cups) fluffy cooked potato

Knob of butter, melted

Large pinch of salt

50g (½ cup) plain flour, plus extra flour for rolling the dough

Method

- Mash the potato well.
- Add the salt and butter.
- Then work in the flour to form a nice dough. Don't overwork the dough, or else the glutens take over and make a nasty cake!
- Divide the dough into two and roll out onto a floured surface.
- Form two circles about ½cm in thickness.
- Cut each circle into quarters (for the traditional look)
- Pan fry for about three minutes on each side, until they have a nice brown surface.
- Dust with flour for effect!

Apple Chutney Breakfast Bap

Serves 2

2 soft floured baps

2 eggs, fried hard

4 rashers of streaky bacon

4 sausages

Knob of butter

Apple chutney

Apple Chutney
Makes 1kg

Perfect to store and use again and again. Also makes a great gift when visiting people!

6 large cooking apples, peeled and diced

3 large onions, diced

60ml (4 tbsp) cider vinegar

60ml (4 tbsp) white wine vinegar

100ml (½ cup) apple juice or cider

300g (1½ cups) sugar

150g (1 cup) raisisn or sultanas

1 tablespoon grated root ginger

2 teaspoons mustard seed or wholegrain mustard

1 teaspoon mixed spice

1 teaspoon cinnamon

2 star anise

Salt and pepper

Lots of jam jars! (3 or 4 is good)

Start with the chutney...

- In a large saucepan begin sautéing the onions until they begin to soften.
- Add the apples and stir for a minute or two.
- Add the rest of the ingredients and leave to simmer on a low heat for about 45 minutes or until you've achieved a nice pulpy reduction.
- Allow to cool a little and place in sterilised jars – it's best that the chutney is still warm when going into the HOT sterilised jars.

For the bap...

- Lightly toast and butter the baps.
- Build it up with the cooked crispy rashers, sausage and fried eggs. Top with a big dollop of chutney.
- The amazing flavour of the salty meat and the sweet and sour chutney – a fantastic combo!

HOW TO STERILISE JARS

TIP: To sterilise jars, place clean jars into a hot oven at 180°C/ 360°F for 10 minutes. Make sure the chutney is also warm and goes into a HOT jar. Then place the lid on securely and voilà you have your very own chutney.

WE'RE SERIOUS ABOUT COFFEE

Before we opened Shells I never really drank coffee. I don't like milk, so I always thought it would be too strong without it. I did envy people that would sit and stir the lovely thick foam of a cappuccino or the smooth milk of a latte. The one thing I noticed was a cup of coffee varied so much from place to place. And I also noticed the disappointment when it's a bad coffee. I always thought how hard can it be? Just make a decent cup of coffee... it's not rocket science after all! But in a sense it is. Coffee is both a science and an art. All the steps have to be right to make a perfect cup.

Here's a few tips on how to make the perfect cup of coffee.

• The actual bean has to be good quality and fresh.

• Only grind the bean to order. Ground coffee only stays fresh for up to one hour, so instead of grinding a whole load of coffee wait and grind for each cup.

• Make sure you are also using the right grind; you can have a fine grind or a coarse grind. The process of filtering the water through the grind is

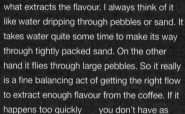

what extracts the flavour. I always think of it like water dripping through pebbles or sand. It takes water quite some time to make its way through tightly packed sand. On the other hand it flies through large pebbles. So it really is a fine balancing act of getting the right flow to extract enough flavour from the coffee. If it happens too quickly you don't have as much flavour and if it happens too slowly then you get too strong a flavour. It has to be just right!

• The same can be said for how much coffee you use. Play around with it and find the right amount for you.

• I always warm the cup first too, as this helps the coffee stay warmer for longer.

• When you get your coffee you are looking for a good crema. A crema is like the skin on top of the coffee; it should be solid and have a lovely golden colour with not too many bubbles. The crema is a real telltale sign of a good coffee.

WHEN IT COMES TO LATTES AND CAPPUCCINOS...

▪ **The most important tip is: Don't burn the milk.** Lattes should be served at drinking temperature. When the milk is steamed to the right temperature, the sweetness of the milk brings out the flavour in the coffee. If that milk is burned, the whole drink changes flavour and you lose the fresh coffee taste.

▪ Always use fresh cold milk and never re-steam milk. I hate it when cafés reuse the same milk over and over again. It's a big no-no. We make sure everyone knows the right amount of milk to use to make one, two or three lattes! That way there's no waste, and each customer gets their drink using only fresh and high quality ingredients.

▪ The last tip is consistency! When you get it right, stick with your method. When people come back to Shells, they come back because they loved it the first time. So make sure it is also as good the second and third time...

HOW WE GET GREAT COFFEE

MASTER ROASTER STEPHEN MACABE EXPLAINS HOW WE GET THE PERFECT BLEND FOR THE CAFÉ.

For Shells we blend three Arabica coffees, from Colombia, from Sumatra and from Brazil. The Brazilian gives a smooth, sweet texture to the coffee, Colombian gives it a bit of a mild acidity and overtones of caramel and nut, and the Sumatran gives it a depth and richness.

We buy the green beans from a broker in the UK and put them through a sorter and sieve. Then the coffee goes into the machine and it takes about 15 minutes for it to roast. It's quite a complex chemical reaction that it goes through. It starts to pop like popcorn. We pay attention to colour, aroma and temperature, but the most important thing is the sound, and that's this popping.

It cools for about 10 minutes before it's packed. It can be difficult for small roasters like ourselves because we're batch roasting about 24kg at a time, whereas the big companies would be doing 30 times that. It's a real skill I suppose that we've built up over the years. It's hand-roasted coffee – this is the real thing – no computers. It's taken a while to be honest to master, but we're there now."
– Stephen McCabe, master roaster

Eggs WHO!?
Eggs Benedict (ham), Eggs Arnold (salmon) and Eggs Florentine (creamed spinach)

Three ways to enjoy your poached eggs, with an easy peasy hollandaise sauce.

Serves 2 to 4

4 organic eggs (the freshest you can find)

4 slices buttered toast

2 tablespoons vinegar

Cress or chives to garnish

Hollandaise:

3 egg yolks

300g (1⅓ cups) diced butter at room temperature

Squeeze of lemon

Topping: Thick sliced ham, organic smoked salmon or Florentine (see variations below)

Method

Place a heatproof bowl over a saucepan of steaming water on a medium heat. (Note: The water in the pot should be simmering, not boiling, but hot enough to melt butter.)

Pour in egg yolks and whisk straight away

Slowly add in the butter – make sure this is done in stages. Whisk vigorously in between. Keep the temperature low and add the butter slowly... the key phrase here is 'low and slow, low and slow'. The eggs must not scramble!

TIP: The aim here is to emulsify the egg and butter together, so you're aiming to melt the butter without scrambling the eggs.

▪ Keep cooking and stirring until the sauce has thickened enough to coat the back of a wooden spoon.

▪ If it gets too thick add a splash of cold water.

▪ Season to taste and add a squeeze of lemon juice for sharpness.

▪ Serve as soon as possible as hollandaise does not reheat well.

Now for the eggs...

▪ Fill a deep saucepan with water and bring to a simmering boil (not rolling).

▪ Add two tablespoons of vinegar and stir to make a whirlpool effect.

▪ Crack the four eggs carefully into the pot.

▪ The whirlpool and the vinegar help to hold the eggs together. Don't overcrowd the pot with eggs.

▪ Allow the eggs to simmer for two to three minutes. You're aiming for a wobbly well cooked white with a runny yolk.

▪ With a slotted spoon, lift the eggs onto a sheet of kitchen paper to soak up the excess water.

▪ Pop the bread in the toaster and when it's toasted, butter it up and top with the ham, salmon or spinach.

▪ **TIP:** For a professional look, cut the toast into circles.

▪ Carefully place the eggs on top and spoon over a generous helping of hollandaise.

▪ To finish, garnish with chives or cress.

The three ways!

Arnold: Fresh organic smoked salmon. We use Burren Smokehouse salmon from Co Clare in the café, and it's a beautiful rich red.

Benedict: Thick slice of baked ham. We bake all our meats in-house in the café, using Irish pork.

Florentine: You'll need a generous pour of cream, 300g (10 cups) baby spinach leaves, freshly grated nutmeg, salt, pepper and a knob of butter. Melt the butter in a saucepan and add the cream. Allow to simmer for a minute or two, until it starts to reduce and thicken. Throw in the spinach leaves and cook for a further two to three minutes until the leaves have wilted. Season with salt, pepper and the grated nutmeg.

Eggcellent Egg and Soldiers

A real nostalgic crowd pleaser, this dish always goes down well at Shells Café. We love to collect eclectic egg cups and little knitted egg beanies. It makes the whole breakfast so much more fun. Lots of our customers hand knit beanies for us in exchange for coffee and cake. Myles' sister was the first person to donate beanies to the Shells cause.

The trick is to use fresh eggs at room temperature and thick-cut homebaked hot buttered toast (see page 126).

Serves 1!
2 eggs at room temperature
4 slices of toast
Butter
Salt and pepper

- Bring a small saucepan of water to a rolling boil, making sure there is enough water to cover the eggs
- Slowly lower the eggs in, to avoid cracking. Make sure you look at the time now.
- For extra gooey eggs: 4 minutes for the ultimate in dunking
- Perfectly soft yellow yolks: 4 minutes and 30 seconds, exactly!
- A firmer yolk: 5 minutes
- Hard boiled: 8 minutes

Remove eggs with a slotted spoon and place in your favourite egg cup. If you don't have one just tear up the egg carton.
Butter the lovely hot toast and slice it into little dipping strips. Crack open the tops of the eggs with the back of a spoon, scoop out the top and season the inside.
TIP: A good variation is to spread a bit of Marmite, fish paste or anchovy butter onto the toast. For an extra treat serve with some crispy dry cured bacon soldiers.
TIP: In spring a great substitute for soldiers are blanched asparagus or even better, grilled asparagus wrapped in bacon.

Yum yum – enjoy.

HOW TO MAKE
EGG BEANIES

Customers are always captivated by the beanies that come on top of soft boiled eggs served at Shells. Keeping a supply of them can be tricky though as they have a habit of wandering away... If you covet these knitted coverings here's how to make a jumper-inspired one of your very own.

You will need:

Wool
A pair of 4mm knitting needles
A button for embellishment (optional)

Method

- Cast on 20 stitches. Work in knit one, purl one rib for two rows. Continue in stocking stitch (knit one row, purl one row) for 18 rows.
- Next row (21 rows) work eight stitches. Bind off centre four stitches, work remaining eight stitches.
- Row 22 purl.
- Row 23 decrease first neck edge.
- Row 24 purl.
- Row 25 decrease one stitch each neck edge.
- Row 26 purl.
- Row 27 (back) knit six stitches, cast on nine stitches (one extra), slip next stitch from left hand needle to right hand and pass extra stitch over, knit to = 20 stitches.
- Continue in stocking stitch for 24 rows. Bind off.

Sleeves:

- Starting on the 13th row, pick up 10 stitches to shoulder and another 10 stitches = 20 stitches decrease each edge (first stitch from edge) on rows five and 11 = 16 stitches.
- Work until 14 rows. Work two rows of knit one, purl one rib. Bind off.

Then cover your egg with the beanie and voilà, the best dressed egg in the village!

Refried Potato Rosti with Kippers, Poached Eggs and Herbs

This is a perfect dish for last night's leftover potatoes, fried up with a delicious oily fish and gooey eggs for a great hangover cure.

Serves 2

300g (1½ cups) cooked crushed potato
2 kippers
Clove of garlic
1 onion, diced
2 large sprigs of parsley, chopped
Lots of crushed black pepper and salt
1 spring onion, chopped
1 large teaspoon dollop of wholegrain mustard
Squeeze of lemon
1 teaspoon capers (optional)
2 eggs, poached

Method

- In a large oiled pan, fry up the garlic and onion until it starts to soften.
- Keeping the pan nice and hot, throw in the potato, flake in half the kipper and the chopped spring onion.
- Add lots of fresh grated cracked black pepper and a dollop of wholegrain mustard – this helps it to bind.
- Let the mix sit for a while and then stir it up again. You're looking for nice crispy brown pieces of potato mixed through your rosti.
- Shape the mix together with a spatula and split into two. Place it on two plates and allow to rest.
- Meanwhile poach the eggs. (see page 44 on how to poach eggs).

To plate up...

- Place the rosti in the middle of the plate and place the remaining kipper on the rosti.
- Carefully balance the poached egg on top of that; you should now have quite an impressive stack.
- Throw on lots of chopped parsley, scattering it everywhere for the ultimate effect (think professional chef at this point) and scatter the capers all around too.
- For the grand finale, season with salt and pepper and a squeeze of lemon juice.
Enjoy!

Open Omelette

with Irish smoked salmon, green peas and dill crème fraiche served with watercress

This is a really easy dish to do. It's a bit different and looks great too – an easy way to impress the loved one first thing in the morning.

Serves 1

3 eggs

75ml (⅓ cup) milk

Salt and pepper

Knob of butter

75g (1⅓ cup) smoked salmon (a few small slices)

A handful of cooked green peas or broad beans

2 onions, sliced, fried and caramelised (keep frying them until they are brown and sticky over a low heat)

Bunch of watercress

Large sprig of dill

Dash of herb oil (see page 108)

Dollop of homemade crème fraiche

Squeeze of lemon

Method

- To start, crack the eggs into a bowl (practice doing this with one hand to look like a pro in front of your friends) and whisk in the milk and salt and pepper.
- Put your oven onto grill to heat up.
- Place a large open nonstick frying pan on a high heat.
- Throw in the knob of butter and melt, spreading it evenly around the pan.
- Slowly pour in the egg mix, listening for a nice 'swoosh' of a hot pan.
- When pouring the egg mix in, make sure to pour into the centre of the pan and allow mix to spread out, this helps get a nice even omelette.
- Add the caramelised onions, most of the peas and slices of smoked salmon.
- Drizzle with herb oil and allow to cook for a minute or two until the edges start to lift from the top of the pan.
- Transfer the pan to under the grill for another min or two until the egg mix is completely cooked through. Keep an eye on it!
- With a flat spatula slowly slide the omelette off the pan and onto a plate.
- Dollop the crème fraiche and chopped dill over the open omelette and scatter the remaining peas.
- Place a bunch of peppery watercress in the middle and a squeeze of lemon all over.
- Season with sea salt and cracked black pepper.

Enjoy!

Big Phat Veggie Breakfast Pie

This is a great family and friends feeder. Make it the night before everyone arrives for a perfect breakfast picnic or for post-surf munchies. Serve cold or hot, whichever you prefer. This dish is healthy, tasty and packed full of veggies.

Serves 8 to 10

Filling

8 to 10 hard boiled eggs, peeled

8 boiled baby potatoes, sliced

4 portobello mushrooms sliced and cooked

300g (10 cups or about 5 large handfulls) baby spinach

4 basil leaves, roughly ripped

1 red pepper, thinly sliced

2 tomatoes, sliced

1 onion, diced

1 clove of garlic, sliced

150g (1⅓ cups) grated mature cheddar

3 eggs and 100ml (1.6 pts) milk, blended to form an egg wash mix

Salt and pepper

Drizzle of herb oil (see page 109) or olive oil

Knob of butter

Wholemeal Pastry

2 eggs

350g (3 cups) plain flour

100g (¾ cup) wholemeal flour

300g (1⅓ cups) cold cubed butter

40ml (3 tbsp) cold water

Pinch of salt

Start off with the pastry:

▪ In a large bowl mix the flour, salt and butter between your fingers to form little crumbs.

▪ Crack the eggs into a cup and add a splash of water. Whisk up with a fork and pour the mixture into the bowl.

▪ Bring the pastry together with a gentle kneading. Turn out onto a floured surface. Shape into a flat ball.

▪ Do not overwork the pastry and leave little blobs of butter as this adds texture to the pastry.

▪ Wrap in cling film and let it rest in the fridge for at least 30 minutes.

▪ Once pastry is cold, roll it out on a floured surface to 5mm in even thickness. Lift and place into a standard 9 inch springform cake tin. Work the pastry with your fingers to build a nice wall to your giant pie.

▪ The pie base is now ready!

▪ Layer the bottom with the sliced cooked boiled potatoes.

Meanwhile...

▪ Preheat oven to 180°C/350°F

▪ Fry the garlic and onions in a pan with a knob of butter, season and add the baby spinach. Allow to cook for about two minutes, until wilted.

▪ Layer the spinach mix on top of the potatoes.

▪ Place the eggs all around the pie. Keep them whole, as this looks amazing when you slice up the pie. The aim is to have one whole egg per slice.

▪ Between the eggs build up the pie with the red peppers, sliced cooked mushrooms, tomato, basil leaves and drizzles of the herb oil.

▪ Pack everything down between the layers and season.

▪ Pour in the egg wash mix and knock the pie around so the mix seeps to the bottom.

▪ Cook in a warm oven at 180°C/350°F for about 40 minutes or until a knife inserted into the pie comes out clean. Make sure there's no runny egg mix; if there is let the pie cook a bit longer.

▪ About 10 minutes from the end of cooking, sprinkle the grated cheddar on top for a golden melted cheese! Yum.

▪ Serve with side salad and homemade red onion marmalade (see page 88).

MARK CAPILITAN

IN THE WAKE OF MAEVE

By Bernie Mongey

Jessie Smith is one of the featured female
riders in a short surf film called *Waking
Maeve*, which was captured over four
seasons in Strandhill.

Jessie is a soul surfer: loving
life: having fun: living in the present
moment. It is this aspect of Strandhill
that hooks people in; they tap into their feminine
side and reconnect with the yin energy of just Being.
Queen Maeve's dominant female spirit of determination,
independence and empowerment has a strong allure. Many
unsuspecting dreamers, find themselves enchanted by the
promise of perfect barreling waves, and are intoxicated
by Maeve's mystical beauty, shrouded beneath the morning
mist. The evening glow that silhouettes her cairn, above
this sacred mountain, (Knocknarea) resonates a spiritual
essence to its people and this place.

It is perhaps this spiritual ethos that influences the
way people here treat each other, and how they live their
lives. Strandhill nurtures a freedom of expression and
individualism that defines this coastal haven. Lifestyle
choices are very evidently fuelled by a passion for the
ocean, shadowed by Queen Maeve's powerful presence,
whose beauty that radiates through inspirational
individuals, like Jessie Smith.

Waking Maeve

My first custom board

Since I started surfing, I've always used Myles' hand-me-down boards. To be honest I was delighted to have a whole selection of boards to surf and never really worried that they may be the wrong dimensions for me. So when we moved to Strandhill and I was surfing more and more, I started to get a real desire to have my own board. I'm not technically minded at all, and no matter how many times people talked about the 'rocker' on a board, or the concave, or any of that spec speak I never got it. I put off getting a board not really knowing where to start.

Then one day around my birthday Myles was being a bit cagey and coming and going from Shells to our house. When I left work that day, Myles made some excuse and ran on ahead. When I opened the door he was standing there holding a 9'6" longboard! It was gorgeous. So shiny and new, with beautiful green and pink stripes. When Myles turned it over, there along the stringer it said "for Jane" – my own custom board. I saw the little Wax On label and Irish flag and felt so proud to have my own board and one that was made less than 10 miles from my local break. I was even afraid to wax it. It just looked so perfect.

Having my own board really made a huge difference to my surfing. At first I was a bit precious but when I got over the fact it was a 'new' board I just took off. There are a few elements I suppose. First of all Myles had told Conor the shaper about my style, my current ability and where I wanted to take my surfing. Also Conor knew the breaks and the kind of waves I would be surfing. So physically the board is a perfect match for both me and the places I surf. But not only that, I felt so good having my own board that I really wanted to do it proud. I also love how it looks, which I know is a bit girly, but that's also a factor too! When you invest in something and love it, it can also change your whole approach.

Since I got my own board I have improved so much. I now can't wait to get another board, and when I do Conor will be my first stop.

ORGANIC SURF WAX

Want to really get in touch with your surfing? Not everyone has what it takes to shape his or her own board, but there's no reason you can't whip up your own organic surf wax. It's only three ingredients and you can obtain two of them locally. Our water here in Strandhill is cold, so this recipe is for the kind of chilly water we've come to know and love.

- Three parts beeswax
- One part coconut oil
- One part tree resin

You can buy or swap your beeswax from your local beekeeper, and take your resin straight from the tree. Tapping a tree to harvest its sap damages the tree and leaves it exposed to pests and disease, so instead study the evergreens in your area. Find a pine that's suffered damage from animals, lightning or wind. You can break off the lumps of sap that have oozed out from any wounds, scars or pruning cuts.

Melt everything together over a low heat in a metal pot. Experiment with ratios to get the sticky factor that you want. And play with your moulds – that's the fun part. Cupcake moulds are pretty cool. Let the wax harden at room temperature or in the fridge. And just like that – you're ready to ride.

Clonakilty Black Pudding and Crispy Bacon Breakfast Salad
Served with griddled Irish Potato Cakes

Clonakilty is a small town in West Cork with a great reputation for black pudding. It also helps that there's a great surf spot just down the road from there too!

BREAKFAST SALAD

Serves 2

4 slices of Clonakilty black pudding

4 rashers of dry cured bacon, cut into small pieces

10 cherry tomatoes cut in half

1 tin white cannellini beans, drained and rinsed

1 bag of mixed baby leaves

2 eggs, poached

SALAD DRESSING

65ml (4½ tbsp) Donegal rapeseed oil

25ml (5 tsp) cider vinegar

1 teaspoon Dijon mustard

2 teaspoons honey

Salt and pepper

Method

- In a hot oiled pan, fry the pudding and bacon until evenly cooked and crispy.
- Pop in the tomatoes and allow to cook for a minute or two.
- Meanwhile, whisk up the salad dressing in a small bowl and emulsify all the ingredients to make a nice sweet dressing.
- Grab a bowl and pop the baby leaves in. Toss in the dressing. Then add the cooked bacon, chop up the black pudding and add to mix.
- Now pour in the beans, give it all a nice swirl and divide onto two plates.
- Next, poach the eggs (see page 44).
- While poaching the eggs, fry the potato cakes in the same pan you used to fry the bacon and pudding.
- Gently place the poached eggs on top of the salad and arrange the potato cakes (see page 41) around the plate.

Enjoy!

Cold Winter Mornings Breakfast Salad

Fruit salad isn't just for summer! Oranges, apples, pears and plums are great to eat in the colder months – no zingy pineapple or mango needed here.

100g (⅔ cup) prunes
75g (½ cup) dried apricots
Soak overnight in a pot of warm water – just enough to cover the fruits.
1 tablespoon honey
1 apple, diced
1 pear, diced
2 plums, destoned
Zest and juice of 1 orange
Small pinch of cinnamon
1 small handful of raisins

- In the morning bring the soaking dried fruit to a slow boil and let them stew for 5 minutes or so.
- Drain and transfer to a cold bowl.
- Add the honey, OJ and zest, cinnamon and raisins to the warm mix.
- Once completely cool, stir in the remaining fruit.
Sit down and enjoy with your favourite yoghurt.

by the sea

Mussels

The beach can be a great place to forage for food – if you know what you're looking for. Get it wrong and you could be in for a bout of something nasty, get it right and you'll be in seafood heaven. To make your way to foodie paradise, just follow our advice on how to collect and cook mussels properly.

Setting off
When foraging for mussels, the general rule is to pick a beach with clean water far from any towns. A nice rural spot is less likely to suffer from pollution than an area adjacent to a big city. Go at low tide, but first check with the fisheries board for general quotas. You've got to respect nature!

Harvest
Bring a nice big bucket and a screwdriver to remove more reluctant mussels. Only pick good-sized shellfish that are bigger than your thumb, leaving the little babies to keep on growing. Never pick open mussels, only the closed ones. If one is partially open, tap it. It should close, but if it doesn't then don't take it. Find rocks that are heavily populated, with nice big clumps of mussels. The lower the tide the better, and the general technique is to twist and pull. Use the screwdriver if needs be.

Transport
Keep your mussels in a bucket that you've filled with seawater. You'll need 15 to 20 mussels per person, and make sure you bring a friend foraging, as the bucket will be heavy on the way home!

Filtering
When you have your quota, keep the mussels out of direct sunlight and in the bucket for one or two hours, as this is when the filtration process happens. Basically your mussels are now filtering the sand out so when you tuck in later there will be no crunchy surprises!

Cleaning
The next step is to clean them. With a blunt knife, rip off the beard – which is the weedy bit – and give the shells a clean to remove barnacles.

Big Steamy Bowl of Mussels

Serves 2

900g (2lbs) mussels, washed, scrubbed and
beards removed

1 small onion finely diced

2 cloves garlic, chopped

100ml (½ cup) dry white wine

50ml (¼ cup) or a large dash of cream

1 tablespoon dillisk seaweed, finely sliced
(optional)

2 tablespoon parsley, finely chopped

2 tablespoons olive oil

Sea salt

Method

- Heat a large pot on a high temperature and throw in the olive oil.
- Add the garlic first and fry until it starts to turn a nutty brown, about 15 seconds, and then add the onions.
- Allow the onions and garlic to cook for a minute or two until they begin to soften.
- Pour in the white wine and let the alcohol boil off. Keep the wine at a rolling boil for another minute.
- Add in the cream, then reduce the heat to medium.
- Add in the mussels. (Make sure you discard any open mussels as these are dead.)
- Next add the dillisk and parsley. Give everything a stir.
- Put a lid on the pot and let the mussels steam and cook nicely until they have all opened. This should take around four to six minutes. (Discard any mussels that have remained closed at this point.)
- Serve with warm crusty bread and a glass of dry white wine.

Variations

- Cook the mussels with leak, spinach and peas for an extra healthy twist.
- Substitute the cream with a tin of coconut milk and a teaspoon of green curry, then throw in some mange tout, lemon grass and chilli while sautéing the onions. This makes an awesome pot of curried mussels.
- Throw in a slug of French pastis as they do in France for that aniseed flavour.

THERE
ARE
OTHER
FISH
IN THE
SEA

- It's really easy to do a bit of mackerel fishing. On a still day when the sea is like a mirror, paddle out – a longboard, kayak or a canoe will do. Put bits of kitchen foil on a hook and you're bound to catch something.

- If you come across a lobster pot that's washed up on shore, take it out with you on a longboard. Be sure you have a working float. Lobsters are easier to catch than you think. Stinky, salty bait is said to attract them best.

- In some parts of the world spear-fishing is cool, but here in Strandhill is a bit of a snorkeling scene. Be on the lookout for sea urchins, small crabs and even lobsters.

- Before you start catching your dinner though, check local laws to see what permits and licenses might be required.

Smoked Mackerel, Parsley and Pearl Barley Salad

Pearl barley is a cheaper alternative to rice and pasta. It is also healthier! It gives a great nutty texture and flavour.

Serves 2

1 full smoked mackerel
200g (1 cup) pearl barley
1 large bunch parsley
About 500ml (2¼ cups) vegetable stock
Salt and pepper
1 clove garlic
1 white onion, diced
Knob of butter
Some tomatoes on the vine, for garnish and colour on the plate

Method

- Rinse and then simmer the barley on a low heat with just enough water to cover it.
- Simmer for around 45 minutes, topping up the barley with vegetable stock until you have a nice, plump juicy barley grain. It should be soft to the touch, slightly al dente to the bite.
- Rinse the barley using a colander. Set aside to cool.
- Place barley into a bowl.
- Pan fry the garlic and diced onion using the knob of butter and season with salt and pepper.
- Toss the garlic and onion mix into into the barley.
- Next wash and de-stem the parsley, then coarsely chop the leaves, keeping some whole for effect.
- Stir the parsley into the barley and onion mix. This forms the base of the salad.
- Next plate up the barley, then flake the smoked mackerel on top.
- Balance a pile of hot crispy onion rings on top for major wow factor! Place the vine tomatoes on the side.
BON APPETIT!

Crispy Battered Onion Rings

Who doesn't like onion rings...?

2 large peeled onions
1 cup plain flour
1 tablespoon flour for dusting
1.5 cups sparkling water
1 teaspoon baking powder
3 dashes Tabasco sauce
1 medium sized pot hot vegetable oil

Method

To begin, grab a medium sized pot and fill with veg oil to about halfway. Heat the oil right up to 175°C/350°F – basically just before smoking stage. Test by dropping a tiny piece of onion in and seeing if it bubbles and sizzles to the top quickly, in which case it's ready.

To make the batter

- Mix the baking powder with the flour and whisk in the sparkling water to form a smooth light batter.
- Sprinkle in a few dashes of Tabasco and stir.
- Cut the onions in a cross section into whole rings.
- Discard the inner rings, as they are too small.
- Use the outer rings, accessing them by pressing out the rings with your fingers.
- On a plate, dust the rings in plain flour and toss them in the batter you have just made.
- Stir around with a fork to ensure they are fully covered.
- When you are satisfied the oil is hot enough, slowly drop in each battered onion ring, using a fork or a pair of tongs.
- After about 10 seconds, the onion should start to float.
- Don't overcrowd the pot and cool in stages for about a minute or two between adding each onion. You are looking for a nice golden colour.
- Rest the onion rings on kitchen paper to drain away excess oil.

Enjoy with mackerel salad, burgers, barbecue or on their own with chilli mayo!

Oysters

Oysters are in big demand and also a vital part of the coastal rural community. Nothing beats a pint of Guinness and sliding back a few oysters after a heavy cold surf. To me, eating fresh oysters is like eating the sea. In Ireland we don't do Tabasco; instead it's a splash of a little onion and vinegar dressing. Personally I keep mine plain, as the seawater taste is what I'm after!

Serves 2

1 small red onion, finely chopped
1 teaspoon sugar
2 tablespoon red wine vinegar
2 cans of Guinness
6 oysters, on a bed of ice

Method
Combine onion, sugar and vinegar together. Stir around and let the flavours marry for a few minutes before serving.

How to shuck an oyster:

- Make sure the oysters are still alive by checking that the shells are tightly closed.
- Hold the oyster in the palm of your hand with a towel, so that you don't accidently cut yourself if the knife slips.
- Make sure the oyster is in your hand "cup side down and flat side up" so that when opened the juices will remain inside the shell.
- Insert a dull paring knife or oyster knife between the 'lips' near the hinge.
- Twist the knife so that the oyster muscle detaches and then peel back the top shell, keeping it steady as not to lose any juices.
- Work the muscle free from its shell with the knife and serve it on the half shell and on top of a bed of ice.
- Serve asap.
- Place the onion mix in a cute bowl alongside the oysters and sprinkle some of the onion mix on, if you desire.
- And don't forget to drink the Guinness, and make sure you let that settle before you eat the oysters…

Poached Salmon and Potato Salad
with Green Beans and Watercress

Poaching is a lovely, healthy and easy way to cook fish. The best fish to poach are salmon or trout. Although you can buy watercress year round, it is an easy one to forage. Look out for it near running water and small streams around springtime.

Serves 2 as a main meal

Serves 4 as a side salad

2 salmon fillets

400g (2 cups) cooked baby potatoes

2 handfuls fine green beans (sometimes called French beans)

1 bunch watercress

1 tablespoon wholegrain mustard

1 tablespoon honey

2 tablespoons mayonnaise

3 scallions (spring onions), sliced thinly

Juice ½ lemon

Salt and pepper

Lemon wedge for garnish

Method

Start by poaching the salmon:

- Bring a small pot of water to the boil and lower the heat so it is just simmering (not a rolling boil).
- Add a few pinches of salt to the water and stir.
- Slide the salmon in and make sure it is fully immersed
- Allow the fish to gently simmer for about five minutes until cooked through.
- With a slotted spoon take the fish out and place on kitchen paper to soak up excess water (but keep the water to cook the beans).
- When cooked, break up the salmon with your fingers into nice large flakes – it should flake naturally.

- With the same hot water, drop in the green beans and allow to cook for a minute or two until 'al dente', or still crunchy.
- Drain and rinse with ice cold water to regain their green colour.

- To make the dressing, use a small bowl and mix together the honey, mustard, mayo and lemon juice. The honey will make the dressing runny.
- In a large bowl, slice the baby potatoes into halves or quarters and stir in the dressing, sliced scallions, salt and pepper.
- Pop a potato in your mouth to see if it needs more of anything, for example seasoning, dressing or whatever you think.
- When you're happy with seasoning, toss the ingredients gently around and stir in the green beans.
- Spoon into a bowl and flake the poached salmon on top.

Next top the salad with lots of watercress.

This dish has lots of lovely tastes and textures going on: the crunch and pepperiness of watercress, silky salmon and the bright beans, along with the sweetness of the mustard dressing… DELISH!

HOW TO GUT A FISH

So you've caught your fish! Take the hook out and whack it on the head. Now it's time to scale and gut it. This is best done outside as it can be really messy work. It's a real no-no to leave fish guts and scales around common fishing areas, so always clean up after yourself no matter how remote you are.

The best way to remove scales is with a blunt serrated knife or butter knives, holding the tail in one hand and brushing the knife from tail to head with hard rasping strokes to chip away the scales. Don't forget the top of the fish and around the head gills and collar, otherwise known as the tastiest parts.

Flip the fish onto a flat surface, hold it down with one hand over the head and back, and insert a sharp pointed knife into the back vent located on the underbelly near the tail. Slice upwards towards the head but be careful not to insert the knife too deep, otherwise you'll puncture the innards. Follow through with a bit more force past the pelvic fins and on up to the base of the lower jaw. Reach inside behind the head where you will feel everything connect; pinch that spot and sweep down scooping out all the nasty stuff. Afterwards check the inside, as you might have to scrape out the liver attached to the backbone.

Removing the gills, which is best done with scissors or a sharp knife, prolongs the freshness of the fish. In some large fish the gills can give it a bitter flavour when cooked, but with smaller fish the gills can just be ripped out. Rinse the entire fish with icy cold water and refrigerate as soon as possible or store on ice until ready to be cooked.

Don't forget to conjure up an elaborate story of catching your fish and how it nearly got away!

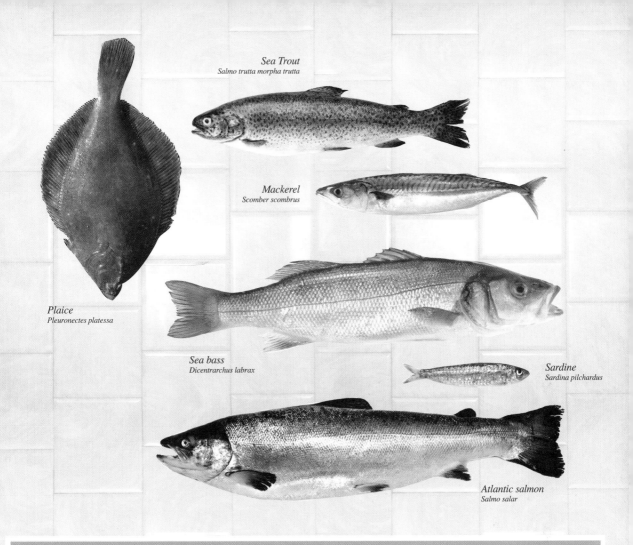

Sea Trout
Salmo trutta morpha trutta

Mackerel
Scomber scombrus

Plaice
Pleuronectes platessa

Sea bass
Dicentrarchus labrax

Sardine
Sardina pilchardus

Atlantic salmon
Salmo salar

FISHY TIPS FROM MYLES

Around Sligo we have the usual catch that you would find all around Ireland. Most common for the sports fisherman are mackerel, haddock, pollock, mullet, cod, gurnard, sea bream, dogfish and – if you're lucky – salmon or trout.

In the café we don't use fresh cod as it's really been depleted from our seas. We often use hake, haddock or a sustainable farmed white fish, and we run mackerel specials every Friday. Of course we use lots of shellfish from all the farms around here too.

When choosing a fish from your fishmonger, go for something different, be brave and try something new like skate (which is brilliant with brown butter and capers) or eel (try this with Chinese greens and fiery horseradish). Often it's a bit cheaper when you experiment and will give you a chance to try out a new recipe.

If the seas have been really rough, chances are there won't be anything too local or fresh available, as fishermen can't fish in really rough seas. Aware of local sea conditions, often I'll go to a restaurant and ask about the catch of the day, knowing that if the weather's been bad it was not caught lately, but was most likely frozen or imported.

Fresh fish should not smell fishy; instead it should smell of the oceans. The eyes are the best indicator: fresh fish eyes should be glossy and plump, not bloody and flat. Fish is best cooked on the bone with the head still attached to give it a fuller flavour. Filleted fish should be cooked lightly, looked after delicately and never overcooked.

Grilled Sea Trout

and Potato Dauphinoise and Pea Puree

Trout is a great alternative
to salmon. Simply cooked under
the grill for a few minutes
it gives you a delicate, light
flavour - which is the best and
only way to eat trout. Trout is
abundant in Ireland, especially
off the west coast, and is more
commonly caught by fishermen
than salmon.

Serves 2

2 small trout fillets, skin on

Splash of olive oil

Sprinkle of salt

Lemon wedge to garnish

For the dauphinoise:

4 to 5 medium potatoes

1 small onion, very thinly sliced

2 cloves garlic

200ml (¾ cup) cream

50g (¼ cup) butter

Salt and pepper

1 standard 1lb loaf tin

¼ teaspoon nutmeg

For the puree:

4 cups frozen peas

1 small onion, diced

350ml (1½ cups) of vegetable stock (stock
cubes are fine)

50ml (3⅓ tbsp) cream

Knob of butter

Salt and white pepper

First make the dauphinoise...

- Preheat oven to 180°C/350°F
- Rub the loaf tin first with a clove of garlic, then liberally with butter.
- Peel the potatoes and slice thinly either with a sharp knife or a mandolin.
- In a large bowl mix together the cream, nutmeg, garlic and thinly sliced onions to flavour the cream.
- Toss the potatoes in the creamy mixture then layer them in the loaf tin, spreading them as flat as you can. Layering the potatoes and onion etc
- Pour in the remaining creamy mixture and squish down with a spatula to pack in all the layers.
- Pop it into the hot oven, then bake for around one hour or until the potatoes are soft.
- In the last five minutes of cooking, whack up the grill to caramelise the top for an extra crispy topping.
- Keep the grill on for the trout.

Then make the pea puree...

- In a small pot melt the butter and sauté the onions until soft.
- Add the peas and vegetable stock and boil as usual. Add more water if needed.
- When peas are cooked, drain away most of the stock keeping back about a third (100ml (½ cup) to 150ml (⅔ cup). Throw this liquid back in with the peas.
- Add the cream to the peas and blend together with a hand blender.
- Taste and season with salt and white pepper.
- You will notice lots of pea pith when you taste it, so now this is the most important step you must do as it makes all the difference: pass the pea puree through a fine sieve (the same one you use to sieve flour when baking).
- Use the back of a spoon to squish the mixture through.
- Make sure you have a bowl handy to catch the puree.
- Now taste again and see the difference... You are now a pro chef!

Trout

- Place the trout on the top shelf under the grill. I keep the oven door open to keep an eye on it. Grill for about three minutes, check it and drizzle a little olive oil on it. Grill for another three minutes or so. Poke a knife between the grain of the fish meat to see if the pink has cooked all the way through. It's better undercooked than overcooked!

On a plate cut out a square of the dauphinoise. Gently place the seasoned trout on top. Smear a spoon of pea puree on the side. Serve with a crunchy side salad of young green leaves and lemon dressing.

SEAWEED

Eat it, drink it, bathe in it or even grow in it, here's how and why!

Most of us think of dry land as the ideal environment for raising vegetables, but in fact the sea floor does a pretty admirable imitation of a garden around these parts. "Seaweed" has been saddled with an unfortunate name; how can something so beneficial be called a weed? We use it in cooking, bathing and even gardening.

The basics
There are three types, generally distinguished by pigmentation. Green seaweed includes Sea Grass and Sea Lettuce, while brown includes Kelp, Alaria and Sea Spaghetti. Red is the most common, and this category comprises Carrageen, Dillisk, Dulse and Nori.

Harvesting
Spring tides are the best times to harvest. Check the tide tables first to make sure to time your visit correctly – the last thing you want is to get caught by the rising sea. As a general advisory, don't overdo it any one area. For example, it's better to take a little bit of Nori from several rocks than to strip one poor rock totally nude. If you're cutting seaweed, then try to take only the upper three-quarters or so from one plant. The bottom part – called the holdfast – is equivalent to the roots you'd find in land-loving organisms, so it's essential to leave this part to carry on living. It's a bit like pruning roses, so give seaweed about three or four months to regrow before harvesting in the same place again.

Culinary and agricultural uses
Coastal communities in Ireland have long harvested the fresh seasonal produce of the sea for use in the kitchen. In fact, the laboratory derived flavour enhancer MSG is a copy of a naturally occurring component of seaweed – so take these tasty seaborne leaves seriously! Carrageen moss is rich in natural gelatine, so use it to set jellies and desserts. It's also a good cure for coughs. Salty Dulse is a traditional flavour additive to soda bread, and to boost the flavour of soups and stews Irish cooks often turn to Kelp or Alaria. Out in the garden, it's worth knowing that before commercial fertiliser came to the fore, seaweed was widely used as a rich soil enhancer. We spread it on our vegetable patch over the winter and leave it to break down for six months. When dug into the soil, it makes our plants thrive.

Baths
Known as the sailor's cure, traditional seaweed baths have been on offer in Strandhill since 1912. We're right next door to Voya, where all the action happens. First, fresh wild seaweed is harvested at low tide. They use what's called toothed or serrated wrack , or Fucus serratus if you want to be scientific about it. This is washed in fresh water to remove shells and grit, then steamed quickly to open the seaweed's pores. Seawater is pumped into the building and heated to a temperature that's just the right balance between scalding and soothing. Into a cast iron bath the hot seawater goes, along with a bucket of slippery seaweed. The combo releases a natural algaeic gel that soothes and moisturises the skin. Luxuriate until life's cares leave you, resting easy in the fact that seaweed contains almost every nutrient the body could ever ask for in its quest to replenish cells and rejuvenate muscles.

BEAUTY FROM THE SEA

The therapeutic properties of wild seaweed have long been known along the Irish coast. At the beginning of the twentieth century there were an estimated 300 seaweed bath houses in Ireland and nine in Strandhill alone. The last of the original Strandhill bathhouses was destroyed in 1961 by the most devastating storm to hit Ireland,

Hurricane Debbie. Fortunately, the Walton family revived this Irish tradition of seaweed baths by opening Voya, which is conveniently located next to Shells. Today their seaweed baths attract over 40,000 visitors every year.

What makes seaweed treatments so special? Seaweed naturally absorbs its nourishment from the sea. As a result seaweed contains countless minerals, vitamins and beneficial ingredients in high concentrations. In fact no plant known has a comparable wealth of mineral elements, macro-elements and trace elements. The mineral fraction of some seaweeds accounts for up to 36% of dry matter.

When seaweed is steamed it produces amazing luxurious oils. These oils – including complex polysaccharides, proteins, minerals and vitamins – are naturally suspended in the water. As heat opens the body's pores, these oils are readily absorbed. The muscles relax and the body is restored, due to the detoxifying effects of the seaweed and recuperative effects of its high mineral content.

Steamed Foraged Cockles or Clams
with Salsa Verde and Garlic Butter

Cockles:

1 large handful of foraged cockles

1 small onion, diced

1 tablespoon white wine vinegar

2 tablespoons dry white wine

25g (¼ stick) butter

Drizzle of oil

For the salsa verde:

2 cloves garlic

2 tablespoons capers

2 tablespoons chopped gherkins

2 large handfuls chopped flat leaf parsley

2 sprigs dill, finely chopped

½ bunch or 2 tablespoons basil, chopped

1 tablespoon of Dijon mustard

200ml (¾ cup) olive oil

Salt and pepper to season

To prepare the salsa verde:

▪ Put all the ingredients together into a food processor and whizz up or hand chop and mix to make a nice thick chunky green paste.

▪ Taste and adjust seasoning with a squeeze of lemon and/or salt and pepper.

To prepare the cockles:

▪ Place a large pot on a high heat, drizzle in the olive oil and sauté the onions, then add the vinegar, wine and butter. Stir around and let this cook for another minute.

▪ Toss in the cockles and put the lid on; shake the pot every minute or so. Cook the cockles for around five minutes.

▪ Divide the cockles into four bowls, dollop a large spoon of the salsa verde on top. Throw a knob of garlic butter on top (see page 157) and enjoy!

Clam, Cockles and Seaweed Vongole

I managed to forage some sea spaghetti (Himanthalia Elongate) for this recipe. It makes a great addition to this dish and it's also great fun if you managed to forage your own clams.

Vongole is a classic European pasta dish. It originates in Venice where they use clams, but as cockles are easier to forage you can use them too. Plus they're just as nice and are actually a type of clam!

Serves 3/4

30g sea spaghetti, or about four or five long, thin strands (don't worry if you haven't got any; the recipe will still work without it)

1 kg (2.2lb) clams or cockles, in their shells, freshly scrubbed clean and all tightly closed

Lots of flat leaf parsley – a whole bunch will do

5 cloves garlic

10 cherry tomatoes cut in half

200ml (¾ cup) dry white wine

Juice of 1 lemon

425g (1lb) spaghetti pasta

Salt and pepper

1 or 2 chillies, depending on how hot you like it

Knob of butter

Drizzle of olive oil

Method

- Soak the sea spaghetti in fresh cold water for a couple of hours. Sea spaghetti is also available in most Irish health food shops and just takes 10 minutes to reconstitute.
- Clean the clams or cockles with lots of fresh water, discarding any that don't close after giving them a sharp tap.
- Put a large pot of water on to boil.
- While the water is heating up do your prep: thinly slice the garlic, chop and destalk the parsley, cut the tomatoes in half or quarters and chop and deseed the chilli.
- Once the water is boiling, throw in the spaghetti and sea spaghetti and cook until 'al dente'.
- While the pasta is cooking, use a wide pan or wok and allow to heat up and then add a drizzle of olive oil.
- Throw in the garlic and chilli and let them sauté for a minute. Pour in the white wine and add the clams or cockles and let them steam with a lid on for around four minutes until the shells have opened and the juices have run out of the shells. (Don't worry if you don't have a lid, you can make one with foil.)
- Give the pan a good toss and then throw in a knob of butter and add the tomatoes.
- Stir and cook for another minute so the tomatoes soften.
- Drain the spaghetti along with the sea spaghetti and toss into the frying pan.
- Mix all the ingredients together and divide into bowls.
- Squeeze a bit of lemon into each one and add a sprinkle of sea salt and some cracked black pepper. Then place a good bunch of the parsley on top.

** it's a very basic sauce to this recipe but there is a lot of flavour that comes out of the clams/cockles. It is a simple dish, that doesn't need any dressing up, the main flavour comes from the clams and that's what you want to preserve.

A BIT OF SURFING HISTORY

By Wayne Murphy.

Strandhill is one of the best surfing beaches in Ireland. To get to Strandhill you have to go past a 300 metre high dome-like hill, Knocknarae, which dominates the surrounding landscape. In the native tongue Strandhill is known as 'An Leathros'. It literally means 'half the headland' (the strand and the hill) and refers to that part of the Coolera peninsula with the magnificent beach in the western shadows of Knocknarae. The big hill is famous as the final resting place for Connaught's legendary Queen Maeve, immortalised forever in the Iron Age epic saga *Táin Bó Cúailnge* (The Cooley Cattle Raid). Kocknarae is also one of the most concentrated areas of megalithic tombs and structures in Europe. Add Ben Bulben and the Dartry ranges into the picture and you certainly have one of Ireland's most spectacular views whenever you look shoreward and paddle for a wave.

BACK IN THE DAY

During the 1970s the Irish surfing scene had changed from a few isolated pockets to a gaggle of thriving surf communities scattered along the known surfing coastline. And of these little surfing strongholds, Strandhill was the most pulsating and liveliest. There in the thick of it was big Stan Burns. A teacher at the girl's convent during the day and a jazz musician by night, Stan also worked in the local lifeguard hut while surfing as much as he could. He was instrumental (no pun intended) in getting loads of youngsters into surfing by sharing all his surfboards and equipment to anyone who looked even remotely interested.

Another musician, James Blenner Hasset, also took to the surf along with others like David Ray. Then the Eniskillen boys led by Grant Robinson, Rocky Allen, Henry and Dave Pearse started to arrive like clockwork every weekend, not just for the surf says Stan, but for the social life as well. "The big gathering place back then was the hotel on top of the hill called The Venue which was run by an absolute lunatic by the name of Kevin Flynn," he recalls. "It was weekend after weekend of music and good times with all kinds of music happening there."

Stan and Blenner Hasset formed a band which became a regular weekend gig. "At the time it was all about having fun. Everyone who surfed in Ireland back then knew each other by first name," he says. "If you drowned it would only be because you were laughing so much. I'd never know who was going to be asleep in my house the morning after a gig — you'd wake up and there would be people on the floor, the sofa and so on." Legendary surfer Barry Britton remembers being a student studying architecture in Dublin back then. "I'd catch the train from Dublin to Sligo every Friday and the lads would pick me up at the station and we'd go to Strandhill for the music and craic that night," he says. "Then we'd head to Easkey to surf for the whole weekend with hardly anyone around."

LADIES ON THE STRAND

Back in the late 1960s and early 1970s Jean Parkes, Helena Conlon and Stephanie Parkes were the first young women to have a crack at surfing at Strandhill. Now there are lots more enjoying the surf there. Some of the better surfers amongst the femme wave brigade there these days are Aine O'Donnell, Clodagh Finnegan, Elisha Hickey, Eliz Clyne, Jessie and Ashleigh Smith and Sarah McGowan. Aine O'Donnell started surfing when she was about 12. "I grew up living by the beach in Strandhill and was lucky enough to have a family who were into the sport and lifestyle," she says. "There were a few girls like Susan McLaughlin, Caroline Flynn and myself who'd surf all year round and I'm pretty sure we used to annoy the pants off the guys with all our antics and chit-chat in the water, but hey, we were having

fun and that's all the matters."

Like all of Ireland's most popular surfi ng locations there have been some noticeable changes at Strandhill since the early days, especially with crowds. Aine O'Donnell says "I remember one recent summer day where I thought to myself — my God, this looks like the Gold Coast of Australia, it was just a sea of black wetsuits, Swell boards and popouts. That was when it really hit home to me that surfing in Ireland had been launched into the stratosphere and there was no going back to the good old days of just you and a few friends in the water. Don't get me wrong, I think it's great to see surfing in Ireland progressing the way it has. The level just keeps getting better because there are more and more people pushing the limits."

STRANDHILL BOYS NEVER PULL OUT

Andrew and Stephen Kilfeather started surfing about 12 years ago and have won numerous surfing and bodyboarding events over the years. Anyone who has seen them surf will attest to their smooth styles and natural grace on a surfboard. It doesn't matter what sort of board either — malibu, boogy, retro, single fin, whatever — these lads have the ability to jump on anything for the first time and ride it as if they surfed it all their lives. "It was inevitable we'd end up in the water surfing because our uncles Bingo, John and Johnston were the full time surf dudes. Guys like Colin O'Hare and David O'Donnell were the hotshots back in the day, along with Conn McDermot and his brother Ross who was an absolute shredder on the bodyboard. The gang I grew up with, Alan, Aron, Steveo and Shambles, are all surfing strong and still loving it.

"These days the beach is infested with groms and they make us feel old. There's a good crew of bodyboarders too. Back in the day it was just myself, Shane and Shambles, but these new youngsters like Rory, Conor, Oran, Errol, Shane, Kevin and David are following in our footsteps and keen for slabby waves further afield. The best thing is that they are continuing with our simple surfing philosophy – Strandhill boys never pull out.

– Wayne Patrick Murphy is editor of Ireland's surf magazine *Tonnta*.

AARON PIERCE

AARON PIERCE

Above: LOCAL, ANDREW KILFEATHER.

Left: COLIN O'HARE'S SURFING AT STRANDHILL HAS INSPIRED MANY UP AND COMING SURFERS OVER THE YEARS.

West Coast Chowder

There are many variations of chowder. Generally speaking, you want a thick, chunky, creamy style soup or stew with your favourite fish. This is the one we make in Shells Café and people come back time and time again for it... It helps that they get to eat it while admiring the ocean!

Serves 4-6

FISH MIX

600g (1½ lb) mixed, diced and deboned fish (Any white or pink fish like monkfish, hake, salmon, ling, seabass, gernard or trout will work, but avoid oily fish like mackerel or tuna.)

200g (½lb) natural smoked haddock or coley

400g (1lb) cooked shellfish (Clams, cockles, razor clams, mussels, scallops, shelled shrimps or prawns and crab will work, but avoid squid or octopus.)

1 tablespoon oil

1 onion, finely diced

1 leek, finely sliced

3 cooked and peeled medium size potatoes, diced

1 carrot, finely diced

2 cloves, garlic

Pinch cayenne pepper (or substitute with a teaspoon sweet chilli sauce)

50g (½ cup) flour

100g (½ cup) butter

400ml (1⅔ cups) milk

100ml (½ cup) cream

Pinch white pepper and salt

600ml (2½ cups) Fish stock

Chopped parsley and chives to garnish

- In a big pot at a high heat, sauté all the veg, except the potatoes, in olive oil until soft to the touch. Set aside in a bowl.
- In the same pot melt the butter and then stir in the flour to make a paste or roux.
- Slowly add the milk and stir vigourly to form a basic thin white sauce.
- Stir in the fish stock, and return the cooked veg, this time adding the potatoes.
- Stir in the cream and the cayenne pepper and chopped parsley.
- Bring all this to a slight simmer and let it thicken slowly, giving it a stir every now and then. This should take between five and 15 minutes depending on the size and thickness of your pot. Keep it on a medium heat.
- Slide in the fish and shellfish and let things simmer for another 10 minutes or so, until the fish is cooked.
- Keep the heat low and avoid stirring so as to not to break up the cubes of fish.
- Take off the heat, but let the chowder sit for another five minutes as the fish continues to cook in its own heat. (Try not to overcook the chowder... cook it slowly.)
- Pour into bowls and garnish with chopped chives and parsley.
- This is even better with brown soda bread (page 130) and a tall glass of Guinness.

Sardine Bruschetta

This is a lovely simple dish that only takes minutes to make, is full of flavour and offers a great source of protein. It's a perfect camping dish too as there is so little prep and cooking involved.

Serves 1

1 tin sardines in olive oil
2 slices toasted homemade bread or toasted thick cut bread
1 tablespoon salsa (see page 117)
Salt and pepper to season
1 clove garlic
Bunch of fresh green herbs such as basil
Lemon wedge to serve

- Toast the bread and afterwards rub a clove of garlic over the toast. This simple approach gives great flavour.
- Build the bruschetta by spreading on the salsa. Next drain the sardines and place on top of the salsa.
- Sprinkle with salt and pepper, top with the basil leaves and serve with a lemon wedge.
- Eat straight away to avoid the toast going soggy from the salsa.

You can pimp it up by adding some al dente green fine beans and some chickpeas. This is great with a glass of cold dry white wine, or a buttery chardonnay.

MICKEY SMITH

SEA WILDLIFE

Here's some of the wildlife we're lucky enough to have around our coast.

Common dolphin

While the biggest concentrations of common dolphins in Ireland are over the continental shelf and in deeper waters, you can also sometimes see these happy-go-lucky guys in shallower water inshore. In the summer, catch sight of them off headlands. The sociable creatures live in herds of up to several thousands and their Atlantic habitat stretches from Newfoundland to Argentina and from Norway to South Africa. Boisterous and vocal, they like to bow-ride boats, ships and even large whales.

Fin whale

The fin whale is the most common large baleen whale observed in Irish waters. These animals prefer deeper conditions along the continental shelf, but they do move within viewing range from the headlands if there's a chance of finding food inshore. The species is the second largest animal living on earth, second only to the blue whale. Seawater shot through their blowholes can reach up to 20 feet in the air, so keep your eyes peeled to see their favourite trick even from great distances.

Basking shark

With elongated gills that stretch almost completely around the head. the basking shark is a passive filter feeder that swims with its mouth open to strain ocean water through its pharynx for plankton. Apparently it particularly prefers ocean fronts where different masses of water meet, since this is where plankton might flourish. At certain time of year, basking sharks do venture into shallow bays almost to the surf line so it's possible to see them from land.

Otter

The Irish name for otter means water dog or hound. The otter is largest member of the mustelid family in Ireland, related to the badger, stoat, pine marten and mink.

Otters have are two layers of fur for warmth and waterproofing, as well as stiff, long whiskers for finding prey in murky water. A set of webbed feet, a streamlined body and a long, rudder-like tail make these furry friends exceptional swimmers.

Seals

In Ireland, grey seal colonies tends to occur on the country's rocky wave-pounded coasts while common seals have an affinity for calmer inshore waters. Both love to dine on marine food, including shellfish, squid, salmon and crustaceans like crab and lobster. Incredibly, half of the entire European population of grey seals is found around Ireland's coastline.

BEACH CLEAN-UPS

We're surrounded not only by breathtaking vistas but also seemingly limitless wildlife. Our local seal colony lives only down the way in Culleenamore, while Brent geese are a stirring sight at Doran Strand. Barnacle geese touch down over the winter at Lissadell, and Oystercatchers – with their distinctive red beaks – are a common sight here in Strandhill. To maintain a pristine view for ourselves and a welcoming habitat for these critters, we're big fans of beach cleans. If you enjoy the seaside, why not host your own event? Here's how.

Planning

Late spring or late summer are good times to organise a beach clean, and two hours is about the right amount of time for your event to last. A Saturday from 10am to noon is ideal, as this gives hungover friends the chance to start the day with some feel-good factor. Be sure to check the diary of events well in advance though; you don't want your beach clean to compete with a successful festival scheduled for the same day.

Promotion

Do tons of publicity. Contact local radio stations and newspapers to get the word out, and call upon a crafty friend to make posters to put up around town. Don't forget to invite the local primary school too.

Expert advice

Environmental charities like the Surfrider Foundation and Surfers Against Sewage are excellent resources. Local reps can offer advice and ideas about publicity. Also get in touch with the council, since they might be able to supply equipment and other forms of support.

Supplies

Obtain litter pickers from the council if they have them, and ask participants to bring gardening gloves that provide protection from sharp objects. Source heaps of regular household bin bags and plastic gloves too.

Logistics

Organise a central registration point. One person with a map should delegate groups to target certain areas. You want to encourage people to spread out, so send the first people to arrive to the furthest point in your patch, then work back as more participants show up. You might assign people to pairs. This means they get to have a chat, and can divide responsibility for collecting recyclables and general rubbish between themselves. Establish several bag pick-up points so no one has to drag their rubbish all the way back to headquarters. A good pick-up point will have road access, as you need to send a van around at the end of the event to carry your collection to the nearest dump.

Incentives

People like beach clean-ups, but you need to give them plenty of reasons – beyond the environmental benefits – to participate. Incentivise the community with the promise of an after-party. A local café can provide sponsorship in the form of tea, coffee, biscuits and cupcakes. Let the local surf shop put on an exclusive screening of a surf film. If your neighbourhood surf school is feeling generous, maybe they can offer free lessons too.

OCEAN CRUSADERS

Help out by helping the organisations who strive to protect our oceans. Here's a few of the organisations working hard on your behalf...

The Surfrider Foundation is a non-profit grassroots organization dedicated to the protection and enjoyment of our world's oceans, waves and beaches. Founded in 1984 by a handful of visionary surfers in Malibu, California, the Surfrider Foundation now has over 50,000 members and 90 chapters worldwide. www.surfrider.com

70percent: 70percent was built to help small groups of friends share knowledge built from years of studying and riding waves and to promote water quality awareness. www.70percent.org/blog

Save the Waves Coalition is an environmental coalition dedicated to preserving the world's surf spots and their surrounding environments. Their goal is to protect surfing locations around the planet and to educate the public about their value. Save the Waves works in partnership with local communities, foreign and national governments, as well as other conservation groups to prevent coastal developments from damaging the surf zone. www.savethewaves.org

Surfers Against Sewage campaign for clean and safe recreational water, free from sewage effluents, toxic chemicals, nuclear waste and marine litter in the UK. www.sas.org.uk

Surfers for Cetaceans call on surfers everywhere to support the conservation and protection of whales and dolphins and other marine wildlife, to protest whaling and the killing of threatened and endangered species, and to end the pollution of our marine environment. www.surfersforcetaceans.com

Sea Shepherd Conservation Society. Established in 1977, the Sea Shepherd Conservation Society (SSCS) is an international non-profit, marine wildlife conservation organisation. Their mission is to end the destruction of habitat and slaughter of wildlife in the world's oceans and to conserve and protect ecosystems and species. www.seashepherd.com

Surfers Environmental Alliance (SEA) was founded by surfers who wanted to do something to protect the ocean, beaches and coastlines, and keep this planet a safe place to surf. If you own a surfboard, enjoy the beauty of the ocean, or if you are concerned about preserving our ocean planet, get involved with SEA. www.seasurfer.org

get out & get going

We love getting out and making the most of the day. From hiking and biking to surfing and strolling... you always feel better after some activity and nothing can beat that fresh rosy glow in the cheeks! Here are some great bites to bring with you for the perfect picnic/ outdoor dining

Beautiful Sandwiches

Here are some lovely ideas for your next lunch if you're getting tired of your ham and cheese sarnies!

For the perfect sandwich bread, follow the recipe on page 126.

Sandwich Fillings

- Roast chicken, basil mayo (add chopped basil to mayo and blend), roasted red peppers and mixed baby leaves
- Handcut ham with apple and mustard mayonnaise (add half a cooked apple and a teaspoon of mustard into two teaspoons of mayonnaise and mix together)
- Herb cream cheese (blend chopped mixed fresh herbs to cream cheese; our favourite in Shells is fresh basil leaves), smoked salmon and pickled cucumbers (see page 88)
- Roast pear, mature cheddar cheese and sausage
- Cheese, strawberry jam and walnut on brown soda bread (see page 130)
- Lemon 'n' artichoke puree with mozzarella and green olives with black pepper
- Curried crab mayonnaise (see below) with iceberg lettuce
- Cheddar and red onion marmalade (see page 88) pan fried toasty
- Avocado, bacon, lettuce and tomato (B.L.A.T.)
- Roast pumpkin and hummus (see page 116) with rocket
- Fried halloumi, avocado and pecan
- Roast chicken, bacon and parmesan cheese
- Strong cheddar, ham and homemade piccalilli (see page 89)

Curried Crab

One thing we're not short of in the west of Ireland is crab! This is an amazing dish and is great served with salad or as a sandwich filler - it's a bit more exciting than plain old crab and mayo.

Makes 6 heaped tablespoons

200g (½ lb) mixed or brown crab meat (generally 2 crab's worth)
170ml (¾ cup) mayonnaise
2 teaspoons mild curry powder
¼ teaspoon hot cayenne pepper (optional)
½ onion, finely diced
1 teaspoon chopped parsley
Salt and pepper
Squeeze of lemon juice

Method:

Combine all the ingredients in a bowl and allow to marinate for a good 15 minutes. This enables the flavours to marry and deepen. Enjoy on a sandwich or even as a starter on top of endive leaves (a type of lettuce that's crispy and liquorice flavoured – perfect with crab), or spread on some crackers topped with cherry tomatoes.

Shells Café Coleslaw

Originally an American salad, Irish people seem to eat coleslaw with everything. Every corner café and restaurant has their version, and here's ours.

Makes 8-12 servings

¼ red cabbage
¼ green cabbage
½ celeriac
4 carrots
Handful golden raisins
300ml (1¼ cup) lemon mayonnaise
3 tablespoons sunflower seeds
2 tablespoons icing sugar
1 apple (optional)

Method

- Combine the lemon mayo and icing sugar together.
- Thinly slice the cabbage.
- Grate the carrots and celeriac and mix in a large bowl. Stir in the raisins, sunflower seeds and cabbage.
- The apple is nice if you're going to serve immediately, but I wouldn't put the apple in if you are keeping the coleslaw for a few days as it 'browns' the coleslaw easily.
- Stir everything together and adjust the seasoning perhaps with a squeeze of lemon juice. Coleslaw should be served cold and crunchy. Best with barbecued chicken!

Mayonnaise

Comparing commercially made mayo to homemade is like comparing cheap shop bought powdered instant coffee to single estate hand roasted espresso pressed coffee. Make it, try it and tell your friends how easy it is. Compare the long list of ingredients on the jar of your favourite mayonnaise to the simple recipe of egg yolks, oil and vinegar... Nothing beats the real thing!

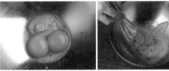

2 large fresh and organic egg yolks
1 tablespoon Dijon mustard
1 pinch salt
1 tablespoon white wine vinegar
250ml (1 cup) oil (a mix of olive oil and nut oil is best)

Method

- Grab a large mixing bowl and place it on a damp folded tea towel for an extra firm base.
- Add the two egg yolks, mustard, salt and half the vinegar, and whisk together.
- Keep whisking very hard and at the same time very slowly drizzle in the oil (feel free to rope someone in to do the pouring).
- You should start to notice the ingredients emulsify; keep whisking vigourously.
- Test and adjust seasoning. If required mix in the remaining half of the vinegar.

Variations

Aioli (fancy word for garlic mayo):
Add a crushed clove of garlic with the egg yolks. For a great depth of flavour add a whole bulb of roasted garlic.

Once made you can add the following to flavour the mayo:
Blended basil, tarragon or dill with some oil.
2 teaspoons curry powder for a spicy flavour.
Tabasco sauce and cayenne pepper to make a hot and spicy mayonnaise.
2 tablespoons tomato sauce to make Marie Rose sauce.
Lemon zest and the juice of two lemons for lemon mayo.
Wasabi paste or grated horseradish for a fiery flavour.

Red Onion Marmalade

A fantastic condiment that goes with almost anything! Put it on your favourite sandwich or serve with a cut of roast meat. It's also great with terrines, pates and salads, and goes amazingly well with cheese.

1 large slug olive oil
12 large red onions, thinly sliced
300g (1½ cup) sugar
100ml (½ cup) red wine
200ml (1 cup) red wine vinegar
100ml (½ cup) sweet red fruity drink,
like port or cassis or even grape juice; I even
used cranberry sauce once, which is great
around Christmas
2 teaspoons fennel seed (optional)

Sweet Cucumber Pickle

900g (2lb) thinly sliced cucumber, unpeeled
3 onions, very thinly sliced
350g (1¾ cups) sugar
Teaspoon salt
150ml (⅔ cup) cider vinegar
100ml (½ cup) water

- Combine the water, vinegar, salt and sugar, and mix until everything is dissolved. Add the cucumber and onions.
- Place the tightly covered container of pickled sweet cucumber in the fridge overnight before using. It should keep up to a week in the fridge.
- It's great with cold cuts of meat, fish or soft cheese.

- On a high heat and using a heavy based saucepan, sauté the onions and olive oil until they soften down and look to be about halfway cooked through. If your onions are really juicy you might want to drain a bit of the liquid – especially if you're making a bigger batch or doubling the recipe.
- Add the rest of the ingredients and give everything a good stir. Reduce the heat and leave the pot uncovered and allow to blip blip away for about 30 to 40 minutes stirring occasionally.
- You're looking to reduce most of the liquid. The onions should be soft so that they break when pressed against the side of the pot with a wooden spoon. Depending on the thickness of your pot, the onions may need a further 10 minutes or so.
- SOFT STICKY SWEET DARK ONIONS MMMMMMMMMMMMM
- Red onion marmalade keeps well in any container for a week or so but sterilised jars are best for maximum longevity.

Irish Piccalilli/ Your piccalilli

Piccalilli is a great condiment, even better when it's homemade. Perfect with cold cuts and a healthier option than a mayonnaise laden sandwich. Make sure to use YOUR favourite vegetable in the recipe. And you need to start this the day before by soaking the vegetables overnight.

Vegetable Prep

- 2kg (4½lb) washed, peeled vegetables

Select from the following: carrots, parsnips, cauliflower, radish, green beans, courgettes, onions, shallots, peppers, celery or any other vegetables that can be eaten raw... (no potatoes then ;-0)

- 4 tablespoons salt
- Water to cover the vegetables

Cut the vegetables into nice bite size pieces and place them in a large container or pot. Cover with water and stir in the salt to make a nice salty brine.

TIP: Place a bowl on top to keep floating vegetables under the brine.

- Leave overnight or for 24 hours. After soaking for 24 hours, drain and rinse thoroughly with cold water.

Now for the Sauce

60g (½ cup) cornflour
20g (3 tbsp) turmeric powder
30g (2 tbsp) mustard (Dijon/wholegrain)
20g (½ cup) ground ginger
1 tablespoon mustard seed
(use less seed if you used wholegrain mustard)
2 teaspoons cumin seeds
2 teaspoons coriander seed
350g (1¾ cups) sugar
100g (⅓ cup) Irish honey
1 litre (4¼ cups) cider vinegar
100ml (½ cup) cold water

- In a large pot bring the vinegar, sugar and honey to a rolling boil, and allow to boil for five minutes.
- Add in the rinsed, prepped vegetables and stir for a minute or two.
- Meanwhile in a small bowl make a paste with the rest of the ingredients. Add to the pot and give everything a big stir.
- Allow to cook for a further three minutes or until the sauce starts to thicken a little.
- The vegetables should still have a nice 'al dente' (crunchy) bite to them.
- Taste and season with salt and pepper.
- Pour into warm sterilised jars and seal. (See page 41)
- Piccalilli is best eaten after four weeks or so, but I can never wait and eat it straight away with a nice ham sandwich. I love it!

LOCAL WALKS

Boots on, Coat on, Flask filled, Picnic ready. Let's go.

It has to be said that in Strandhill we love our walking. It's the easiest way to stay fit, enjoy the great outdoors and – perhaps most importantly – earn a buttered scone with jam as well as a fortifying cup of tea. These are our favourite regions to ramble.

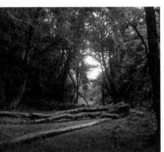

The Glen

To reach this secret forest spot in the lee of Knocknarea, take the Top Road out of Strandhill toward Killeenduff. Turn left when you reach the sharply rising Glen Road. As you continue down this road, a fairy path will appear on the right that seems to lead into a green tunnel. Follow the muddy byway, ducking and diving until you pop up into The Glen, a majestic natural cathedral. Possibly caused by two tectonic plates separating, the grassy channel seems to have been gouged in the rock. Trees have grown here over the centuries, and their vaulting boughs cut this serene space off from noise and time.

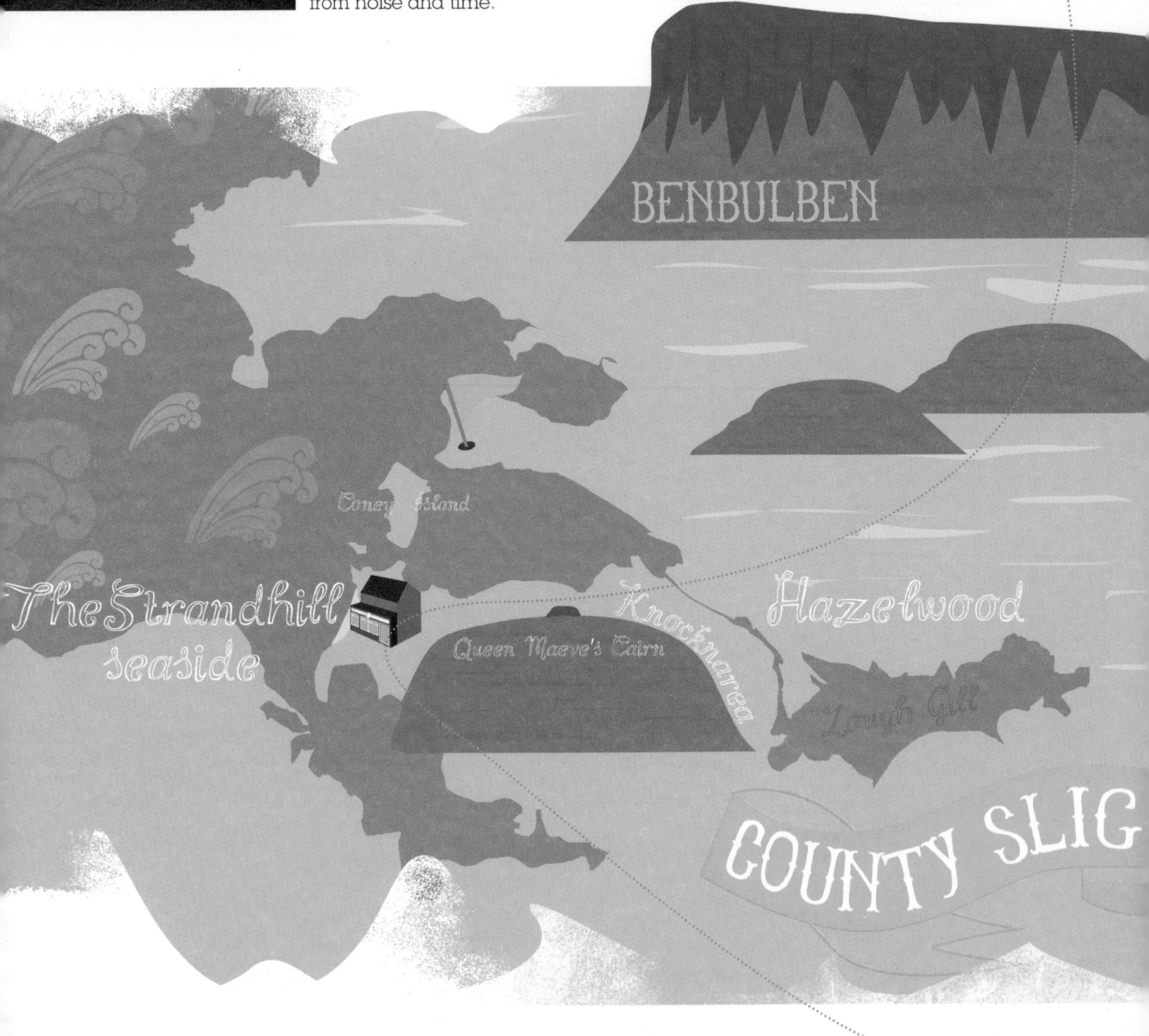

BENBULBEN
Coney Island
The Strandhill seaside
Knocknarea
Queen Maeve's Cairn
Hazelwood
Lough Gill
COUNTY SLIG

The Strandhill seaside

From Shells, carry on along the seafront in the opposite direction from the airport. There are 4km of sand dunes for you to traverse leading to Shelly Valley. From here continue to Culleenamore Strand, where at low tide you can harvest mussels from the rocks and hunt cockles with your bare toes. Then join the Top Road. This takes you back into town to complete your circular walk.

Hazelwood

This well-known mature forest is a family friendly recreation area found in the half moon bay at the northwest end of Lough Gill. A 3km nature trail winds through a canopy of leaves, while info points along the way reveal secrets of local birdlife and identify trees including Douglas Fir, Yew and native Broadwood.

"I love being Irish and that connection with the land that has been here for centuries."

Queen Maeve's Cairn

Hike to the top of Knocknarea, the loaf shaped limestone outcropping that hulks over Strandhill, and you'll reach the rumoured burial site of the formidable Queen Maeve of Connacht. The summit is 452m and takes an hour to reach. From there you'll have 360-degree views, which take in the mighty swoop of Benbulben and Ox Mountain. A 24m cairn rises up to mark feisty Maeve's final resting place. The first century BC warrior queen is said to be buried standing up facing in the direction of her enemies in Ulster wearing full armour with a spear clenched in hand.

MARK CARPILTAN

our
four legged friends

Flask of Veggie Soup

Flasks aren't just for tea and coffee... I've even eaten spaghetti out of a flask! They are totally underutilised, especially in these colder climates...

This recipe makes two litres but keeps well for a few days. In fact the flavour deepens and develops with time. You can also pop the leftovers in the freezer – but only do this once the soup has cooled down completely.

1 tin haricot or cannellini beans
1.5 litres (6⅓ cup) veg stock
1 large onion, thinly sliced
1 fennel bulb, thinly sliced
2 carrots, diced
2 stalks celery, including the leaves, finely chopped
1 tin chopped tomatoes
½ bulb garlic, finely chopped
100ml (½ cup) olive oil

SEASONING
50ml (¼ cup) soy sauce
5 dashes Worcestershire sauce
1 tablespoon sugar
2 tablespoon parsley, finely chopped

Method
In a large pot sauté the onions and garlic with the olive oil. Then pour in the rest of the veg and tinned beans. Don't forget to throw in the bean juice. Stir to mix all the ingredients and allow all the veg to heat up a little, sweating it all for 10 minutes or so. Basically you want to cook the veg to extract the flavour before you add the bulk of the liquid. This is building the base for the soup. Next add in the stock and ensure all the veg is fully covered. Allow to simmer for 10 minutes. Add the soup seasoning, stir and taste. Simmer for another 30 minutes or so until all the veg is soft to the touch and breaks easily. Spoon into the flask and serve a few hours later on the top of your favourite mountain!

Courgette and Almond Soup

50g (¼ cup) butter
1 onion, peeled and chopped
1 potato, peeled and chopped
600ml (2½ cups) vegetable stock, chilled
3 courgettes, finely chopped
25g (4½ tbsp) ground almonds
125ml (½ cup) double cream, plus extra to serve
125ml (½ cup) milk
Flaked almonds (toasted), to serve

Method
Melt the butter in a large pan. Add the onion and potato and cook over a very high heat for five minutes. Add the stock, bring to the boil, then reduce the heat and simmer for 20 minutes or until the potato is cooked. Add the courgettes, bring back to the boil and simmer for five minutes. As soon as the courgettes are cooked, remove the pan from the heat and stir in the almonds, cream and milk. Puree in a blender or use a hand blender to smooth out the lumps and bumps! Reheat gently and season to taste. Serve topped with a few toasted flaked almonds and a dash of cream.

ACTIVE LIFESTYLE

Life's too short to do something you don't like and only get outside at weekends. We made a decision that whatever we ended up doing, our lifestyle would come first. Our sense of freedom and fun is what brought us to Shells, but all the same we have to be careful not to get swallowed up in our work. After all, work is nothing if it doesn't support what makes you happy!

Yoga

When we finish a Bank Holiday weekend at Shells we feel physically spent, but with a few yoga poses you can feel the pressure easing immediately. And with surfing, where you're throwing your body around quite a bit into different positions, stretching out your muscles is important to prevent injury. Yoga's a really great way both to stretch and to escape your mind. Here in Strandhill where everyone is quite fit, it's practically a way of life. The scenery is amazing so you see people practicing in the dunes, right in the natural environment. You feel you just have to be a part of it.

Vanessa Byrne, yoga teacher

Strandhill is really active, really young. I feel like the community here is really positive. There's just something a little bit different from other small villages. From a yoga point of view, it's beautiful to be able to practice outside, like on the highest dunes on the beach. You're overlooking the water and the surfers. It's nature at its best and you're taking full advantage of everything it has to offer."

Cycling

We're so lucky here to have mountains right next to the coast. The mountain biking scene here is a bit underground, so there are secret trails to discover. Nearby Union Woods and Knocknarea have good paths and some steep drops. Of course this is Ireland, so you have to be prepared to be covered in mud. Although we're adrenaline junkies, there are easier cycling routes to pursue too when the waves have gone flat. The coastal paths and leisure trails reveal tiny country lanes, little harbours and cool hamlets.

Kayaking

Although we've travelled quite a bit, we're adamant that you don't have to plan a massive expedition to the Himalayas to indulge your sense of adventure. Around here are countless lakes, rivers, hidden bays and natural lagoons. Kayaking is an excellent way to see them when the surf's gone flat. We sometimes take out a map, point to a river or lake and say, "I wonder if we could paddle that?" And then it's a matter of grabbing the boat and jumping in. As a bonus, it's easy to take a fishing line and bring home some mackerel.

MARK CAPLITAN

YEATS COUNTRY

There's no figure in literature more closely associated with this region than William Butler Yeats. Born in Dublin and educated there and in London, Yeats spent his summers at the family's summer house at Connaught. He developed a deep relationship with the west of Ireland, returning to its myths, themes and landscape for inspiration throughout his entire life.

As a founder of the Irish Theatre – which later became the Abbey Theatre – he served as chief playwright. His more famous plays include The Countess Cathleen (1892), The Land of Heart's Desire (1894), Cathleen ni Houlihan (1902), The King's Threshold (1904) and Deirdre (1907). While his Nobel Prize for literature in 1923 paid tribute to his dramatic works, afterwards he focused more and more on poetry. Among his best-known volumes are The Wild Swans at Coole (1919), Michael Robartes and the Dancer (1921), The Tower (1928), The Winding Stair and Other Poems (1933) and Last Poems and Plays (1940).

We're fortunate to be only a short distance from The Yeats Society, founded in Sligo Town in 1958 to honour the memory of this prolific writer and local hero. The Society operates from the Yeats Memorial Building overlooking the River Garavogue. His final resting place is well worth a visit too; you'll find it just as he wished – "under bare Ben Bulben's head in Drumcliff churchyard".

According to Yeats himself, the "world is full of magic things, patiently waiting for our senses to grow sharper". We couldn't agree more. To start your relationship with this legendary man of letters, take a look at our list of five favourite poems, all of which make reference to this stunning part of the world where we live.

- Under Ben Bulben
- The Old Age Of Queen Maeve
- The Lake Isle of Innisfree
- The Stolen Child
- Red Hanrahan's Song About Ireland

PHOTOS RADKA

On the west coast, you can't wait for the sun to shine or the rain to stop... so just layer up and get out. Soak up the scenery, take a hike, pick some cockles, just go. Free the senses and the spirit in the wind, rain, sun or snow and be inspired by the beautiful countryside, just like Yeats was.

summer time

The shorter the distance between the garden and the table, the better the flavour of the food you make. Let's face it – nothing tastes quite so good as the produce you've grown yourself.

Longboarder and organic gardener Jess Smith grew up teetering on the side of Benbulben before studying at the Organic Centre in Rossinver, so we quickly realised there could be no better person to help us put into practice the art of self-sufficiency at Shells. She planted the organic beds behind the café, and these – along with her patient green fingers – keep us in salad leaves and herbs all summer long. We asked her to share her top tips for organic growing.

Healthy soil makes healthy vegetables. Use composting, manure, mulching, seaweed and leaf mould to save your food from chemical contamination.

Seaweed is loaded with trace elements and nitrogen. I blanket the beds with a generous layer of seaweed in winter and dig it into the soil in spring.

Ideally your veggie patch should face south. If there's a road bordering your property, plant a hedge to filter fumes and toxins from passing cars.

Upcycle a bookshelf if space is tight. Balcony gardeners can lay a bookcase down on its back. Drill drainage holes and fill with soil to create a self-contained bed that comes with readymade dividers.

Grow stuff you want to eat. There's no sense raising anything that you might let go to waste. Think about the recipes you like to make and build your garden plan from that.

Use companion planting to battle predators. Calendula attracts ladybirds, which handily eat up the tiny interlopers that snack on your plants. Marigolds keep greenfly and whitefly away, while nasturtiums repel all kinds of bugs. Plant borage to attract bees; their tiny electric blue flowers are edible and add a pop of colour to summer salads too.

Welcome a nettle patch into your garden. Nettle stimulates growth in plants living near to it. This stinging

your tomatoes a good start.

Upcycle soda bottles to make cloches. By cutting large plastic drink bottles in half, you can make miniature greenhouses that protect any small seedlings you've just planted in the soil from getting too cold.

Herbs are easy and offer good bang for your buck in the kitchen. Plant mint, rosemary, coriander, parsley, dill and lemon balm. Mint should be in a container; it's slow to get going but once it starts it won't stop so be wary of it taking over the rest of your plants. Rosemary is very hardy, almost like a tree, so put it in a corner where it can establish itself.

Harvest summer herbs for winter use. In late summer you might find yourself with quite a lot of both coriander and parsley. The best way to preserve them is to wash the leaves and stalks, let them dry, chop finely, then pack into ice trays. By adding a bit of water before freezing them, you'll have cubes of herbs to toss into wintertime dishes.

Sow cut-and-come-again salad leaves. We plant seeds indoors in March and April, then plant them out in late May. Be sure to give lettuces plenty of space; air should be able to circulate between the plants and between the leaves. When it's time to eat, only trim the outer leaves, leaving the centre part intact.

Pull up plants when they go to seed. At this point a plant is telling you that it's ready to clock off, and you don't want seeds scattering all over your beds. Plus, all the energy is now being diverted to the cause of procreation, sapping the flavour of what you'd otherwise harvest to eat.

miracle worker also speeds up the breakdown of compost, so chuck some in with rotting kitchen waste and garden clippings.

Comfrey "tea" makes amazing plant food. Cut comfrey almost to the base of the plant, then put this armful of goodness into a bucket of water. To keep the leaves and stems submerged you may need to put a weight on top. After a month, the liquid is ready to use. Pour the tea onto the base of plants and watch them thrive!

Fresh comfrey is great for tomatoes. When you're planting a tomato seedling out into soil, dig a hole and put fresh cut comfrey leaves into the hole first. As this subterranean secret ingredient breaks down, it gives

EAT WITH THE SEASONS

January
Carrots • Kale

February
Leeks • Savoy cabbage

March
Spring greens

April
Cauliflower

May
Rhubarb • Asparagus

June
Strawberries • Broad beans • Peas

July
Cucumber • Lettuce • Cherries

August
Raspberries Plums

September
Runner beans • Courgettes

October
Sweetcorn • Apples

November
Potatoes • Red cabbage

December
Brussels sprouts • White cabbage

salads

What an amazing feeling to grow your own salads! We set up a beautiful herb and salad garden out the back of Shells last year. Ok, it was hard work, but it's just so great to pick the lettuce and serve it straight away in a salad. It was a learning curve; some things worked and some didn't. Things like mint, rocket, parsley, cos lettuce and chives really bloomed, but for the life of us we couldn't get basil or softer leaves to grow. It really is trial and error, so start small and learn as you go. We were lucky as we had Jessie to set it up with us, so we had a great start. We also had access to seaweed from Voya's seaweed baths next door, an amazing natural and organic fertilizer.

Here are a few tips to get you going!
Get seeds at your local organic centre or order them online, but make sure they are organic.

THE LEAVES:
Rocket: great peppery taste
Lambs lettuce: soft and sweet, looks great on the plate and such a cute name
Baby pak choi: thick and juicy
Tatsoi: glossy and green
Mustard leaf: packed full of sharp flavour
Winter purslane: delicate little leaf
Red chard: great colour, earthy sweet flavour
Baby spinach: earthy green flavours

If you're tight for space, you can always do a herb box, even on a raised platform. Saves your back from all the bending over and weeding! Grow the classics: basil, rosemary, coriander, thyme, sage, mint and dill. And if you're feeling confident, these are some great herbs with good flavours to try: tarragon, oregano, lemon balm, applemint, chervil, chives, lovage and sorrel.

Start at your local organic centre or order them online, but make sure they are organic

Surfers Salad

This salad makes a great pre-surf lunch; it's fresh, healthy and tasty too.

Serves 2

2 large handfuls mixed baby leaves
4 slices halloumi cheese
1 ripe avocado, diced
Handful walnuts
8 cherry tomatoes, halved
½ cucumber
1 slug olive oil
Honey mustard dressing (see page 107)

Method

- First prep your honey mustard dressing.
- Peel and cut the cucumber in half lengthways and run a teaspoon down the middle to 'deseed' the cucumber; cut this into elongated thick slices at an angle.
- In a hot griddle pan, toss in the walnuts and heat through to give them a toasting. Put to one side.
- In the same pan, drizzle in a little olive oil. When nice and hot, fry the halloumi cheese one minute on each side.
- Build the salad with mixed baby leaves, tomato and cucumber. Gently place the avocado on top with the halloumi cheese and finish with the walnuts.
- Drizzle with honey mustard dressing and enjoy!

West Coast Salad

This salad has great flavours and fantastic colours. We also show you how to 'supreme' an orange, a handy tip to have.

Serves 2

1 small packet wild rocket
4 small precooked beetroot
1 orange
50g (⅓ cup) feta cheese
Balsamic reduction (page 109)
Tablespoon almond flakes

Method

▪ Quarter the beetroot and toss around in a bowl with a drizzle of balsamic reduction.
▪ Build the salad with rocket leaves, beetroot, orange segments and cubed feta cheese (a nice hard goats cheese will also do).
▪ Drizzle some more balsamic and a scattering of flaked almonds.
▪ To make it more beautiful, add a few edible flowers – so summery so fresh!

How to 'supreme' an orange

• Using a serrated knife, strip the top and tail off the orange.

• Now that you have a flat surface on the orange to work with, use the knife to trim off the skin as well as the pith (the white stringy bits), making sure you just have the flesh of the orange left.

• You will notice white lines, or pith, between each segment. Insert the knife as close as possible to the membrane surrounding the segment and cut down the centre and do the same on the other side of the segment to release the segment with no pith.

• You will be left with a tender orange segment.

• Continue with the rest of the orange to release all the segments.

Perfect Caesar Salad

You find it on many restaurant menus but few places get it right. You must be a lover of anchovies or else it's just not the same. Here at Shells café, we use pickled anchovies instead of the stronger tasting salted variety.

Start by making the croutons:

15g (1 tbsp) butter
2 tablespoons olive oil
2 slices slightly stale bread crusts, diced

- Melt the butter in a hot frying pan and add the olive oil.
- Toss in the bread and cook until the croutons are golden all over. Watch the heat – if it's too hot you might ruin the croutons.
- Depending on the soakage of the bread you might want to add a drizzle of olive oil.
- Scoop out and drain croutons on kitchen paper and let them cool.

For the dressing:

50g (2 oz) tin anchovies, mashed
2 egg yolks
1 clove garlic, grated
Juice of 1 lemon
½ teaspoon Dijon mustard
2 dashes Worcestershire sauce
Pinch ground black pepper (no salt needed, as the anchovies add the saltiness)
150ml (⅔ cup) vegetable oil and 75ml (½ cup) olive oil, mixed
50ml (¼ cup) cold water

- Place all the ingredients in a bowl except the oil mix and water. Stir around to make a paste with a whisk.
- Keep whisking vigorously and slowly drizzle in the oil mix.
- Keep whisking and slowly whisk in the water to make a pouring consistency. This dressing can also be made in a food processor, but remember the oil and water must be drizzled in slowly.

To build the salad:

Serves 2

1 large bowl Cos or Romaine lettuce
1 handful homemade croutons
50ml (¼ cup) homemade Caesar dressing
12 pickled anchovy fillets
Parmesan shavings (from a good quality parmesan, never use the powdered variety, which will ruin your salad)
No bacon, no chicken, no tomato or cucumber... keep it simple and high quality

- Slice the lettuce into strips and toss into a bowl.
- Now add the croutons
- Pour in the dressing, just enough to coat the leaves.
- Stir in some grated parmesan cheese, about one tablespoon.
- Split into chilled bowls or plates. Place about six to eight anchovies on each salad and another drizzle of dressing. Add some phat shavings of parmesan using a vegetable peeler.

Salad Dressings

These are often overlooked but can greatly improve the flavour and taste of any salad. Have fun and experiment with dressings – you'll be surprised what you can make!

▪ A general rule is three parts oil to one part vinegar. Add something herby, tangy or sweet.

▪ For a good base oil mix, try 50% olive oil and 50% groundnut oil.

▪ Other great oils are rapeseed oil, avocado oil and walnut oil. We sometimes use sesame oil, but be warned it's a little stronger than the others. Great with beef and duck salads though!

▪ The best vinegar to use is white wine vinegar or a good quality cider vinegar. I love trying flavoured vinegars too, like tarragon or raspberry vinegar. If you're looking for a darker dressing, then use balsamic vinegar. This is also great to use with Italian dishes.

▪ Malt vinegar is too strong and will overpower the dressing. Lemon juice is a great substitute for vinegar in dressings as it adds that sharpness.

▪ To mix the dressings I like to use an old jam jar with a screw-top lid. Bang it all in and give it a good shake.

▪ If I'm using garlic or anchovies – that is, something a bit more solid – then I blend it using a hand blender. Often I'll season with salt and pepper and a teaspoon of sugar or honey.

Basic Vinaigrette

(serves 4-6)

200ml (1 cup) oil (olive)
65ml (¼ cup) white wine vinegar
Salt and pepper

▪ Combine and whisk or shake well and serve immediately.

Now it's time to play with the ingredients

▪ Garlic vinaigrette – add crushed or grated garlic to your taste
▪ Lemon and herb
▪ Lemon, lime and chilli
▪ Lime and grated ginger
▪ Garlic, mustard and herb – add a teaspoon of mustard and teaspoon of herb with grated garlic
▪ Lemon, garlic and herb
▪ Lime, ginger and chilli with coriander
▪ Honey and wholegrain mustard – use cider or balsamic vinegar, one teaspoon of mustard and a teaspoon of honey
▪ Orange, honey and Dijon mustard
▪ Orange, ginger and honey
▪ Basil and garlic with balsamic
▪ Orange and basil dressing
▪ Mint and basil dressing – use cider vinegar
▪ Crushed raspberry dressing – add a teaspoon of white sugar
▪ Crushed raspberry and mint dressing
▪ Crushed strawberry and black pepper dressing – use raspberry vinegar
▪ Crushed strawberry and basil dressing with balsamic vinegar

▪ You can also add cream, mayonnaise or yoghurt to a dressing but cut down the vinegar quantity to avoid curdling – use a squeeze of lemon instead, then add:
▪ Blue cheese, for Roquefort dressing
▪ Parmesan cheese, for Caesar dressing
▪ Hot mustard
▪ Wasabi paste
▪ Horseradish
▪ Curry powder
▪ Garam massalla
▪ Toasted fennel and coriander seed

Flavoured Oils

In Shells Café we love to combine herbs with oils, and basil oil is the one we use the most.

Balsamic Reduction

This sticky sweet black substance is used a lot in many restaurants and a nice addition to the earthy flavours found in salads.

500ml (2 cups) balsamic vinegar
100g (½ cup) sugar

In a tall pot, boil the vinegar and stir in the sugar. Keep boiling until two thirds of the liquid has reduced. Test the consistency by drizzling a small amount on a plate and leave for a minute to make sure it has reached the tacky syrupy stage. Store in a bottle or jar.

Basil Oil

1 large bunch of basil
500ml (2⅓ cups) extra virgin olive oil
¼ teaspoon salt

- Blend ingredients together for at least three minutes with a hand blender.
- Looks great drizzled over the top of any food, or on the plate in a circle around the food.

Spring Onion Oil

This one is used widely in Hong Kong.

4 spring onions or scallions, thinly sliced
200ml (1 cup) olive oil and 200ml (1 cup) sunflower oil, blended together

- Heat up the oil in a small pot until nice and hot. Throw in a piece of scallion and if it quickly sizzles to the top it's ready.
- Throw in all the chopped scallion and cook for 30 seconds.
- Take the oil off the heat and let it cool.
- Spoon the scallion oil onto your lunch. This goes great with cold meats and fish.

Chilli Oil

We love this oil as it adds another level of flavour to any dish.

450ml (2 cups) groundnut oil or sunflower oil
50ml (¼ cup) sesame oil
5 dried chillies, split down the middle

- Put the chillies in a saucepan and pour in the oil to gradually heat through. Don't overheat or it will taste bitter.
- Turn off, allow to cool a little and pour into a sterilised bottle.
- A more fun way to make chilli oil is to open up a glass bottle of oil, pour a little out and pop in your split chillies. Screw the top back on tightly and put it through the dishwasher at 80/90 degrees. Voilà – chilli oil!

Super Green Healthy Oil

1 bunch watercress, chopped
400ml (1¾ cups) olive oil
Pinch salt

Blend together into vibrant thick green oil. Looks fantastic!

Curry Oil

2 teaspoons cumin seeds
2 teaspoons coriander seeds
2 teaspoons mustard seeds
1 teaspoon whole pepper
1 teaspoon dried chilli flakes
1 teaspoon garam masala
400ml (1¾ cups) sunflower oil or groundnut oil

- Toast all the spices in a hot pan; keep the pan dry and fry for just a few minutes. Put them into a pestle and mortar. Crush into a pulp or whisk up with a hand blender.
- Meanwhile heat the oil gently. Pour in the mixed herbs and stir. Allow to cool.
- Pour into sterilised bottles and enjoy!

WE LOVE BARBECUES

MYLES'S TOP TIPS FOR MAKING A GREAT BARBECUE

Being South African, I've grown up around barbecues, although we call them braais. Since no one in Ireland uses the word braai, I've had to change my ways!

▪ You must have a decent bag of charcoal. It's a bit pricier than briquettes, but definitely worth it. And none of this gas barbecue talk either! For me that's a big no-no.

▪ Get a good kindling fire going, by starting with small pieces of dry wood and a little bit of firelighter to help get the flames going. Pour this over the charcoal.

▪ A fire needs three things: fuel, heat and oxygen. People often forget the oxygen part. The fire must have oxygen to breathe, and this comes in from the bottom. So if needs be, give three hard blows to the base of the fire. Watch out for singed

eyebrows though!

▪ After a good 20 minutes the coals should be white hot. Use this heat to burn the grid, removing any debris from your last barbecue. Perfect – you never have to wash it!

▪ Now you need to test for heat. Hold your hand 10cm above the coals. If you can't hold your hands over it to the count of five, then it's still to hot to cook on and the food will just be burnt. Wait it out until the heat is perfect and you can reach a count of five holding your hand over the flames.

▪ The rule of thumb is: meat on the bone first (such as chops) and processed foods last (such as burgers and sausages).

▪ If you're cooking fish, cook this last as you want low heat. Also use a swivel grid, which locks the fish inside a grid, so you can flip the fish

quickly and easily.

▪ Don't play with the food too much; allow it to cook and only turn once.

▪ If the fat is dripping off and causing big flames, move the fatty cuts of meat to the side instead. Throwing water on the fire will only result in lots of ash being dispersed onto the food, which is not great. If you have to, raise the grid up a bit instead.

▪ If you are having a large barbecue, start a second fire about 30 minutes later; that way you'll always have a supply of hot fire.

▪ Always, always keep the barbecuer in supply of cold beer! It's hot work and they need to be looked after. This tactic also means you'll probably get the prime cuts of meat…

Enjoy!

SOME COOL THINGS TO TRY ON THE BRAAI

Toasted sandwiches
Buttered on the outside and preferably done in a swivel grid.

Butternut squash
Take a butternut squash, slice in the middle, remove pips and stuff with hummus, then wrap in tin foil and throw in with the coals. Needs to cook for about 40 minutes and should be turned once.

Large whole onions
Leave the skin on, as the skin protects the onion. Throw directly into the coals. They will be black as soot, but peel that skin off and tuck in for some succulent onions. This is what's so cool about barbecues – very little prep, waste or packaging. Just great whole foods that can take the flavour of real coal. It's also an involved way to cook, with everyone standing around drinking and chatting.

Marshmallows
No matter how young or old, everyone loves roasting marshy! Make sure you gather the roasting sticks before it gets dark though.

Garlic bread
Check out the flavoured butters on page 157 and spread on the crusty bread, wrap in foil and place on the grill for about 15 minutes, turning halfway.

Veggies
Don't forget vegetarians. It's easy to do some great vegetable skewers, just keep the vegetables chunky. Nothing beats some grilled asparagus, topped with a little butter and seasoning. Delish!

Drinks
You'll need beer, and lots of it! If you're feeling adventurous try making homemade lemonade (page 122) or knock up a simple fruit punch. Just mix three parts cheap red wine, one part fruit juice, chopped mixed fruit and about one part lemonade.

Big Beefy Burgers

Have a crack at making your own gourmet burger. It's cheap and easy, and it will definitely impress your friends when you say you made them yourself. You can put your own little twist or character into your bespoke burgers. I like to use coriander seeds in mine but you can add pink peppercorns, black onion seeds or horseradish. A big no-no (and I've seen it done a hundred times) is to put a big dollop of tomato sauce into the burger mix, because this will burn and blacken your burger very quickly thanks to the high sugar content.

TO MAKES FOUR LARGE BURGER PATTIES, YOU'LL NEED:

800g (2 lb) top quality mince, not too lean since you want the fat for flavour

1 small onion, finely diced

2 cloves garlic, finely diced

2 tablespoons parsley or coriander, finely chopped

1 teaspoon coriander seeds

1 teaspoon Cajun spice

1 tablespoon Worcestershire sauce

1 teaspoon wholegrain mustard

1 egg, to help bind everything together

Salt and pepper

- In a large bowl mix all the ingredients together. Roll up your sleeves and give everything a good squelch around with your hands. Divide into four and roll out into giant meat balls of around 200g (7oz) each.
- Roll out some cling film and place a meatball on top. Give it a gentle push down with the palm of your hand to form a nice looking pattie, then wrap it in cling film, give it a further slap down to get it nice and flat and pop it into the fridge until ready to use. Grill on high heat until the juices run clear and not too pink. Enjoy on a toasted bap with crisp lettuce, tomatoes and pickles.

Burger alternatives
- 50% beef 50% pork mince lends extra flavour.
- Handcut your mince beef; buy a good steak and dice the meat fine.
- Why not try venison, ostrich or even a bunny burger?
- My particular favourite is a lamb burger with tzatziki.

Grilled Salmon Burger

Fish burgers are a healthier option and a refreshing change to
the norm. This is a quick and easy dish that tastes amazing.
Great when all your friends are up for the weekend, crashing in
your house and robbing your best boards!

Serves 2

2 x 200g (½ lb) salmon fillets, marinated in shop-bought teriyaki sauce
Crunchy cos lettuce
4 tablespoons pickled cucumber (see page 88)
2 tablespoons mayonnaise combined with 2 tablespoons horseradish
2 ciabatta rolls, grilled warm and buttered

- On a hot griddle or barbecue, cook the salmon fillets. Generally this should take three to five minutes, as the salmon goes from translucent orange to a nice dusty pink. Don't overcook the fish!
- Meanwhile prep the buns with the horseradish mayo on both sides.
- Next add a layer of cos lettuce for a crispy crunch.
- Using a spatula, gently place the fish on top of the lettuce. Scoop on lots of pickled cucumber and dollop on a bit more horseradish mayo. Top the burger off with the other side of the roll, and push down giving the burger a food squeeze so that the juices flow down! Tuck in and enjoy.

The Best Chicken Burger

... like ever!

Serves 4

4 large Chicken breasts, 200g (½ lb) each
4 floured baps, Portuguese rolls or ciabattas
3 tomatoes, thickly sliced
8 thick slices good Cheddar cheese
Basil Mayo (see page 87)

- Prep the chicken breasts by carefully slicing the chicken with small lacerations to open up the breast for a flatter burger look.
- Bash the chicken with a meat clever, a wine bottle or rolling pin. This softens and spreads the chicken.
- Place into a large bowl.

For the marinade:

100ml (½ cup) rapeseed oil
4 cloves garlic, diced
Sprig of rosemary, chopped
100ml (½ cup) white wine
Juice and zest of two lemons
300g (1¼ cup) plain thick yoghurt (optional)
Cracked black pepper
Pinch of cayenne pepper

- Combine all the ingredients of the marinade and work into the chicken breasts. Allow to marinate for at least two hours or preferably overnight.
- Place the chicken breasts on a hot barbecue grill or in a hot pan. Cook each side for about four minutes.
- To build the burger, use a soft bap, roll or ciabatta. Dollop on some basil mayonnaise, then add a layer of crisp iceberg lettuce. Next place two thick slices of ripe tomatoes on top. Now add the cooked chicken breast and put on two thick slices of cheddar and more basil mayo. Let the burger rest for a minute or two and then tuck in!

BUILD A BURGER

Let you imagination run wild with different combinations.

THE BASICS:

- **Get the textures right.** You want a good outer casing, such as a sesame roll, ciabatta, Portuguese roll, soft flour bap, wholemeal roll or cheese roll.
- **Then you need a good crunchy lettuce.** It's not everyone's favourite part, but essentially you need that crisp, cool, juicy crunch. Iceberg is best or try the likes of cos, la rossa, rocket or butter leaf.
- **Tomato gives a nice, sharp, sweet flavour that cuts through the grease of the burger.** It also adds another flavour level. The lettuce and tomato combo are great – just look at the ever popular BLT.
- **For meat, it's definitely worth sourcing through your butcher.** You may pay a little extra for it, but it's worth it for the extra quality. Fat content is important. Too lean and you'll lose flavour, too fatty and it will be soggy and greasy. A great tip is to use 40 percent pork and 60 percent steak mince. The pork will leave a pinker colour, but don't be turned off as it will add a lovely sweetness to the burger patty.
- **The big cheese.** We find a mature cheddar works best. Don't scrimp and use plastic cheese please! Other great cheeses are soft cheeses like goats, brie, swiss, mozzarella and even blue cheese or haloumi. Avoid sweet cheese like Gouda though.
- **A tip for cooking burgers:** place the cheese on top and place a metal bowl or dome-shaped lid over it. This will melt the cheese super quick.
- **To bacon or not to bacon?!** It's better to bacon. Use dry cured or smoked or even try a crispy chorizo instead.
- **Extra toppings make your burger unique.** Purists go with onions, pickles and tomato ketchup, but really anything goes. Here are some of our favourites...
- Fried eggs, deep fried pineapple, onion rings, grilled onions, caramelised onions, salsa, guacamole, red onion marmalade, banana chutney, fruit chutney, tomato relish, barbecue sauce, homemade mayonnaise, mustard mayonnaise, wasabi, Japanese pickles, tzatziki.

Hummus

A great accompaniment to any barbecue! Here's a basic recipe with loads of options to give it a twist. Quick and easy to make, it keeps well or can be eaten straight away.

HUMMUS BASICS

2 x 400g (1¾ cups) cans chickpeas

¼ cup liquid from the cans

Juice of 1 lemon

2 teaspoons tahini paste (sesame paste)

2 cloves of garlic, diced

Large pinch of salt

4 tablespoons olive oil

1 teaspoon ground cumin

- Drain the chickpeas and set aside the liquid from the can.
- Combine all the ingredients in a food processor and blend.
- Add the liquid from the can last to adjust the consistency.
- Blend for another minute until nice and smooth.
- Taste and season with salt and pepper, lemon juice or more cumin or garlic depending on your taste palate.

Options

- Roast Beetroot Hummus: Blend in two small cooked beetroots for a radical purple hummus. Looks pretty amazing!
- Roast Red Pepper (same as above)
- Roast Pumpkin with toasted coriander and cumin seed
- Herby Hummus: Try adding rosemary, thyme, tarragon, basil or lemon balm and mint. Just add the chopped herbs when blending all the other ingredients. Two tablespoons of herbs should be plenty.
- Hot Hummus: Dried chilli or cayenne or even throw in a fresh green chilli – this is fantastic!
- Lemon and Mint Hummus: Add the juice and zest of one lemon and chopped mint.

Marinated Tomato Basil Salsa

4 large tomatoes, chopped into eighths
½ punnet cherry tomatoes, a different colour or variety
½ red onion, finely diced
8 to 10 basil leaves, thinly sliced julienne style (thin strips)
1 tablespoon flat leaf parsley, chopped
1 teaspoon balsamic vinegar
1 teaspoon sugar
1 red chilli, deseeded and thinly sliced
4 tablespoons extra virgin olive oil
1 teaspoon coriander seeds (optional)
Salt and pepper

▪ Combine all the ingredients together in a nice pretty bowl and allow to marinate at room temperature for at least 20 minutes.
▪ Be sure to taste before serving and season if necessary.

Myles's Guacamole

If your avocados are not soft to the touch... don't bother!

2 RIPE avocados, mashed with a fork
Juice of ½ a lemon
1 teaspoon ground cumin
1 clove garlic, finely grated
Salt and pepper
3-4 dashes Tabasco sauce (depends how hot you like it)
Dollop of crème fraiche

▪ Mash all the ingredients together with a fork. It can get messy so start off in a big bowl and transfer to a cute bowl for serving.
▪ Squeeze some lemon juice on top of the guacamole to slow down the browning process. But it's best to serve immediately!
TIP: To ripen the avocados – keep them beside some bananas or place them in a black bag on the window sill.
TIP: To bulk up the guacamole add some chopped tomatoes, fresh coriander or chopped chilli for extra heat.

FORAGING

Fred Symmons is an environmental consultant and wild food addict, forever hunting down mushrooms, shellfish, game, plants, berries and fish in County Sligo. In summer he might bring us samphire, which we swap with him for a cup of coffee and a slice of apple pie. He's even been known to deliver a lobster to Myles as a present, for which we rewarded him with an order of fish and chips. Most foragers don't give away their secrets, but our favourite scavenger is a generous kind of lad, so here are the tips he shares for setting off on your own wild food adventure.

Fred Symmons, forager

"In Sligo we're blessed with wild food. I've always lived this rural life and seen this amazing bounty, but I wasn't sure how to make it available to myself. Through reading and actually just getting out there and doing it, I taught myself.

You have this added sense that comes alive when you're foraging. There's nothing better than finding a big, plump cockle sticking out of the sand and putting it in your pocket. When you get back to the car your pockets are drenched, but you've got your dinner.

You could be looking up at a tree and see nothing, but if you change the angle and keep the sun out of your eyes you'll start seeing nuts appear from nowhere. You want to get them before they fall. If you miss it by a day, the squirrels have got them.

That's the key of the forager: once you've got the eye for a plant, you memorise it. Write a few notes: When did you find it? Where did you find it? For me it's the feeling that if all the shops closed or there was a food shortage, I would have the skills to survive. There is a bounty there, but most people walk past, totally oblivious to it."

FORAGING FOODS

Beechnuts
Collect these from late September. Excellent and sweet, but a lot of work. You have to pick-peel them, and one out of every five usually hasn't dried out properly.

Bilberries
Late in summer all the woods around Lough Gill have wild bilberry, which is what blueberries originate from. Most people walk through thinking it's just heather. With persistence and a couple of hours you can get enough to make a pie.

Blackberries
Anyone can find blackberries in the hedgerows when summer ends and autumn is on the way. It's a good idea to pick them slightly under-ripe so you get more pectin and sharpness.

Elderflower
The elder tree smells like a tomcat has been let loose on it. When the white flowers come out, make a cordial or freeze them. They're beautiful with gooseberries.

Hazelnuts

Make a wild pesto using hazelnuts, wild rocket and garden mint and parsley. It's fantastic, the best of the best.

Meadowsweet

In May and June start looking for these flowering plants. You can make teas, cordials and various concoctions.

Pennywort

Also known as Navelwort, this grows all over the stone walls on Ox Mountain. It's a very crunchy green that's good in a salad.

Samphire

Samphire comes up late July and into August. Know where the beds are and keep an eye on them. It's such a humble plant that you'd hardly see it unless your eyes are trained. The Queen orders it with her salmon.

Sea beet

As we move into summer, sea beet comes into its own. It's the precursor to all root vegetables like carrots and parsnips. Find it along the foreshore. It's there for only a couple of months and then it's gone.

Sea lettuce

As a foraging food, sea lettuce is great – it looks like lettuce! Find it in clean rock pools and use in soups as a thickener.

Sea spaghetti

Very easily recognisable – this is the seaweed with long thin strands. Mix it with linguini and fettuccini. It's a great partner and you wouldn't know that it's seaweed.

Wild strawberries

Find these in July or August up Knocknarea. Peel back the grass, nettles and brambles and find the gorgeous leaf and little scarlet berry that looks like it's dried up and shrivelled. Put it in your mouth and you'll never eat shop-bought strawberries again.

FRED'S TOP FORAGING TIPS

Seasons are key. It's not like going shopping in your supermarket. Something might only be available for a couple of months and then it's gone. But when it's there it's like treasure visiting you each year.

Get a good book. This is one of the keys to all foraging. Richard Mabey's Food for Free (Collins Gem, 2012) is a life-enhancing classic. The Wild Food Yearbook (Kelsey, 2006) has everything. And Edible Wild Plants and Herbs (Grub Street, 2007) by Pamela Michael is a beautiful book.

Start with the basics. Go for the obvious first and start building up a picture of what's out there.

Be careful not to collect where dog walkers go. That's one word of wisdom. You don't want to go stepping in or harvesting around what the dogs have left behind.

Get the thrill of finding your own food. And then find uses for it.

Gradually build up a mental map. This tells you from season to season where things are likely to be.

It's a relationship with nature. Never take more than you need.

Homemade Jam or Fruit Compote

There's a lot to say about jam making and I'm sure your distant aunt can give you a zillion handy tips, but here at Shells we make the simplest fruit compotes and they go down very well.

2kg (4.4 lb / 14 cups) (frozen) fruit berries (eg strawberries, raspberries, fruits of the forest, blueberries or gooseberries when in season)
1kg (5 cups) white sugar
A splash of water (100ml) (½ cup)
Small knob of butter
Juice of 1 lemon

Method

- Grab the deepest pot available and on a high heat throw in the (frozen) fruit.
- Next add in the water and stir around as the fruit begins to soften and melt.
- Add in the white sugar and give the mix a good stir.
- As everything begins to melt, dissolve and come together, squeeze in the lemon juice.
- Allow to boil for 20 to 30 minutes watching that it doesn't boil over. Keep stirring every now and then.
- If a foamy scum forms, throw in a knob of butter, as this helps to prevent the foamy build-up.
- You're looking for a thick and syrupy fruit consistency. When cooled it will thicken up. If you have a sugar thermometer it should be between 105°C/220°F and 108°C/225°F.

To test to see how it will set grab a cold plate and with a spoon spread a thin layer of the fruit compote onto the plate. Give it a minute to cool. You can now feel the consistency that you want. If you want extra thick jam, boil it for longer to reduce the liquid.

- Take it off the heat and allow to cool for a little in the pot.

Sterilised jam jars are the best for storage (see page 41) but Tupperware is also fine.

As there are no preservatives the jam will only last a few weeks, unlike shop-bought ones.

Other fruit compote Ideas:

Rhubarb and Vanilla
Plum and Ginger
Blackberry and Apple Jam
Peach Compote

NOTE: This should make about six standard jam jars – one for your neighbour, one for your sister and four for yourself!

LABELS

There's nothing nicer than homemade jam, marmlades and chutneys so why not have homemade labels too? Here's some labels for you to photocopy or just download them from www.thesurfcafecookbook.com

Cordials!

It's so rewarding to make your own cordial — full of fresh fruits, some that you've foraged. Once they're stored in a sterilised bottle and kept refrigerated, these cordials can last up to three months. It's so impressive to invite your friends round on a summer's eve and kick back with fresh homemade lemonade. Even better to add a drop of rum or vodka to some of the mixes... and hey presto the party's just beginning.

The best mixer to use is soda water, but sparkling water is fine too. Add lots of ice and cool glass and a straw.

Lemonade

Makes 300ml

3 lemons, juice and zest
150g (¾ cup) caster sugar
150ml (⅔ cup) water

Method:

Place the sugar and water in a saucepan and bring slowly to the boil, stirring to dissolve the sugar. Boil for two minutes. As it cools mix in the juice of three lemons and the zest. The more zest you use the better! Pour into glasses, top with ice and add soda water, and serve immediately with fresh mint! This is a summer favourite at Shells. (Not a favourite in the kitchen as we have to zest over 17 lemons! But it's always worth it in the end.)

TIP: Zest the lemons first (before squeezing) with a fine grater.

Raspberry Fizz

Makes 4 glasses/1 jug

300g (2½ cups) raspberries
3 tablespoons sugar dissolved in 2 tablespoons hot water to make a sugar syrup
1 litre soda water
4 sprigs mint

Method:

▪ Mash the raspberries with a fork and add in the sugar syrup. Mix around so all the sugar is dissolved.
▪ Pour into four glasses with ice and slowly top up with soda water. Top with a fresh raspberry and a sprig of mint, then serve!

Warning: This is delicious with a splash of vodka and a drop of cassis... And I believe all the vitamins in the raspberries help stave off a hangover!

Elderflower Fizz

Even better with your own foraged elderflower! The season is short as they only bloom once a year between the end of May and the second week of June. Ask a local where to find the elderflower bushes off the beaten track, as I'm cautious about harvesting them on the roadside where they could be drenched in petrol fumes and covered with pollution. Don't forget to pick some for your house too... and to garnish the drink. They're such a beautiful delicate flower with great flavour.

6 to 8 heads of elderflower
175g (1 cup) caster sugar
600ml (2½ cups) cold water
2 lemons, juice and zest

Method:

Put the sugar and water into a saucepan over a medium heat. Stir until the sugar dissolves. Add the elderflowers; bring to the boil for five minutes, remove from the heat and add the zest and juice of the lemons. Leave aside to cool. Cover and leave to infuse for 24 hours. Strain and bottle or serve.

TIP: This is great with gin!

make me, bake me

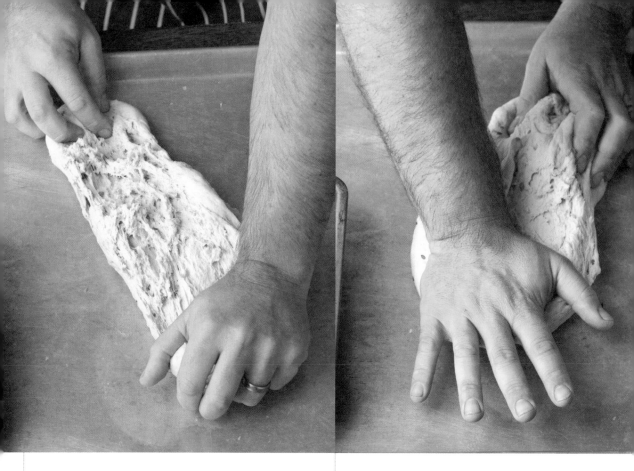

- Preheat oven to 200°C/390°F
- Place all the dry ingredients in a mixer. Chop butter into small cubes, add to dry mix and mix until blended in. Don't worry if you don't have a mixer, you can use your hands and a lot of upper body strength instead!
- Add water to the mixture. As soon as the dough comes together, remove from mixer and knead until the dough is smooth.

- Kneading the dough is about pushing and pulling the dough using the palms of your hands. The goal is to form elasticity.
- Place in a large bowl with a small drop of oil in the bottom of the bowl. Cover tightly with clingfilm and leave to rise next to or on a warm oven for about 45 minutes.

The Best Sandwich Bread

We've only given this recipe for one loaf, as unlike shop bought bread it has no preservatives and therefore needs to be eaten same day or next day at the latest. But believe us, this is so worth it! You will need 'strong flour' which can be bought from most supermarkets. Don't substitute plain flour for strong as you will end up with crumbly bread.

Makes 1 loaf

540g (4⅓ cups) strong white flour

20g (1⅔ tbsp) dry yeast

1½ teaspoon salt

40g (2 tsp) sugar

80g (½ cup) seed mix

20g (1½ tbsp) butter, cubed

300ml (1¼ cup) warm water (if it's too hot you will kill the yeast, too cold and it will not grow)

Splash of oil

- Then remove from the bowl and knead again for a further five to ten minutes, until the dough is smooth. Shape the dough to fit in a loaf tin.
- Place the dough into a well oiled loaf tin and leave over the hot oven to rise for around 30 minutes. Be careful not to allow dough to over-rise. It should be just over the top level of the loaf tin.

- Cook at 200°C/400°F for approximately 30 minutes.
- Remove from the tin for the last five minutes of cooking time.
- Test by tapping the base of the loaf. It should sound hollow.
- Leave to cool on a tray before slicing.

Jane's Mum's White Irish Soda Bread

Traditional Irish Soda Bread does not contain any fruit, eggs or fats such as butter or margarine. There are just four simple ingredients required: flour, bread soda, buttermilk and salt. But you need the right simple ingredients to get the best results.

Irish flour is different. It's made from wheat grown in a particular soil and climate, and is soft and low in gluten. If you can't get Irish flour, use all-purpose flour but do not use hard or bread flour. These flours are very high in gluten and simply will not work in breads that do not use yeast.

Don't overlook the importance of the buttermilk. Ordinary milk will not do – it is the high acid content in buttermilk reacting with the alkaline bread soda that causes soda bread to rise.

Phil's secrets to great soda bread:

- No kneading, none is required.
- A light touch – use only your fingers rather than your full hand to mix the dough.
- Work fast and get it into a hot oven the minute the dough is shaped.
- The reaction between the buttermilk and the bread soda starts the instant the ingredients meet (if you can't get hold of buttermilk, use runny natural yoghurt instead). That's why it is vital to get the bread into the oven without delay – you want this magic reaction happening while the bread cooks. Wait too long and the reaction is all over before heat is applied and your bread will not rise.
- It's very important to have everything ready before you begin and then get on with it as quickly as you can.

450g (3⅔ cups) Irish white flour (or unbleached or all-purpose flour)
1 teaspoon bicarbonate of soda (bread soda)
1 teaspoon salt
500ml (2 cups) unhomogenised buttermilk
Preheat the oven to 230°C/450°F. Do not start until the oven is hot.

- Sieve the flour, bread soda and salt into a large bowl and mix. Make a well in the centre of the flour and pour in about two-thirds of the milk. Quickly and with a light touch bring the flour in from the edges and mix with the milk, until all the ingredients come together into a dough. Use your hands for this, never a spoon or mixer.
- The exact amount of buttermilk needed will depend on the nature of the flour. Judge by the look and feel of the dough, which should not be sticky but should come together easily into one piece of soft, slightly floppy dough.
- If it's too dry and crumbly add a little more buttermilk; if it becomes sticky, add some more flour.
- Once the dough has come together, do not knead, simply place it on a floured wooden board, pick up a handful of flour and rub it into the palms of your hands so that they are perfectly dry, and shape into a flat round about two inches thick.
- Place on the baking tray, and then cut a large x on the top. This results in more even cooking.
- Do all of this as quickly as you can, from start to finish should take less than five minutes. Then put the bread into the oven immediately.
- Wait for about five minutes and then turn the oven down to 200°C/400°F.
- The initial high temperature ensures a good crust. After another 20 minutes take the bread out and knock on the base. If it sounds hollow it's done, if not pop it back in for about five to ten minutes and then check again.
- The bread should be eaten the day it is made. (This will not be a problem!)

Brown Soda Bread

This makes three loaves. Brown soda bread lasts for ages and in fact often tastes better the next day. You can also freeze this and defrost it just before your friends arrive for a weekend of surf. The same rules apply as for white soda bread; don't use strong bread flour and don't overmix it.

675g (5⅔ cups) brown stoneground wholemeal flour
225g (1¾ cups) plain flour
1 tablespoon brown sugar
4 tablespoons sunflower or vegetable oil
2 tablespoons bicarbonate of soda (bread soda)
1 teaspoon salt
750ml (3¼ cups) buttermilk
1 tablespoon golden syrup
1 tablespoon treacle or mollasses
1 tablespoon of your favourite seed mix

- In a large bowl mix the dry ingredients together.
- In a separate bowl mix the wet ingredients together and pour into the dry mix.
- Stir together lightly to form a soft dough or batter.
- Do not overmix; keep as much air in the mix as possible. This is very important.
- Divide into oiled loaf tins.
- Sprinkle the seed mix on top and pat down gently with the back of a wet spoon.
- Bake for 45 minutes at 180°C/350°F.
- When baked, pop the bread out and cool on a wire rack.
- For a softer crust place a damp tea towel over the bread as it cooks.

Banana Bread

Makes 1 loaf

225g (1¾ cups) self raising flour
½ level teaspoon salt
100g (½ cup) butter
175g (1 cup) caster sugar
100g (⅔ cup) sultanas
50g (½ cup) chopped walnuts
100g (½ cup) glace cherries, washed and patted dry (optional)
2 large eggs
450g (2 cups) ripe bananas, mashed. The blacker the bananas the better; ripeness = flavour.

Method

- Sift the flour and salt together, then rub in the butter until the mix is like breadcrumbs.
- Add sugar, sultanas, walnuts and cherries.
- Mix together and make a hollow in the centre.
- Crack in the eggs and the mashed bananas.
- Beat all the ingredients thoroughly.
- Line a buttered loaf tin and pour in mixture. Spread evenly.
- Bake for one and a half hours at 180°C/350°F.
- Test with a skewer in the middle of the loaf and see if it comes out dry.
- Cool before removing from the tin.
- Banana bread done!

Irish Whiskey Pudding

This is comfort food at its best and it's a great alternative to fruit pudding. Friends who have claimed to hate fruit puddings have licked their bowls clean after eating this.

Serves 6

250g (1¾ cups) dates, roughly chopped
250ml (1 cup) water
5ml (1 tsp) bicarbonate of soda
100g (½ cup) butter, softened
200ml (1 cup) caster sugar
1 egg
250ml (2 cups) plain flour
5ml (1 tsp) baking powder
100g (1 cup) pecan nuts, chopped

FOR THE SYRUP:
250ml (1 cup) sugar
120ml (½ cup) water
120ml (½ cup) Jameson Whiskey
5ml (1 tsp) vanilla essence
30ml (¼ stick) butter
½ teaspoon ground cinnamon

Method

- Preheat the oven to 180°C/350°F and grease an oven-proof dish.
- Combine the dates with the water in a small pot and bring to the boil. Remove from the heat and add the bicarbonate of soda.
- Cream together the butter, sugar and egg. Sift the flour and baking powder and add to the creamed mix together with the cooled dates and mix well.
- Mix in the nuts and pour into the greased dish. Bake for about an hour or until a skewer comes out clean.
- For the syrup, boil the sugar, water, butter and vanilla essence together for about 10 minutes. Add the whiskey and cinnamon and mix well.
- Serve the pudding with the syrup poured over it and top with some whipped cream, or custard if preferred.

AFTERNOON
TEA

Zingy Zingy Lemon Cupcakes

Cupcakes require equal quantities of butter, flour, sugar and eggs. So if you want 12 cupcakes it's 200g (1 cup) of each and four eggs, or if you want 24 cupcakes it's 400g (2 cups) of each and eight eggs. The most popular flavours are lemon or vanilla, so either add lemon zest or vanilla essence. Don't limit yourself though; feel free to add chocolate powder or fresh blueberries.

A good tip is to make sure the butter is very very soft. This helps it combine with all the ingredients and not leave chunks within the buns.

Makes 12

CUPCAKES:
200g (1 cup) self raising flour
200g (1 cup) butter
200g (1 cup) caster sugar
4 eggs
Zest of a lemon

EXTRA LEMONY FROSTING
100g (½ cup) butter
200g (1 cup) icing sugar
1 egg white
Juice of a lemon

Method

- Preheat oven to 180°C/350°F. Cream the butter and sugar together. Your aim is to dissolve the sugar into the butter. Slowly add in the eggs and pop in the lemon zest. Sieve in the flour and fold into the mixture. Don't overbeat.
- Spoon the batter into paper cupcake holders. Only fill halfway, leaving room for the cakes to rise.
- Bake for 15 to 20 minutes.
- To make the frosting, whisk all the ingredients together to form a nice paste. It's pretty easy when using a hand blender. Season to taste. Thicken it with more icing sugar or add more lemon for tartness.
- Once cupcakes are cooled, spoon or pipe on the frosting.
- A nice touch is to add some candied fruit sweets.

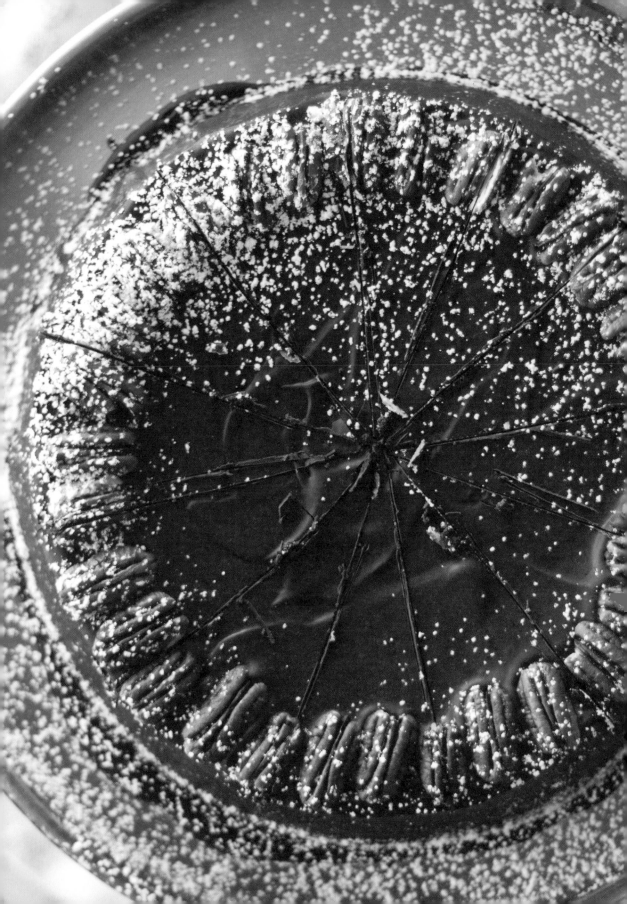

Flourless Chocolate Cake

Extra rich and easy to make, this is a great one when you have a large group around for tea as there's sure to be someone with a wheat intolerance. This recipe is great as the cake will keep well for a good few days.

Serves 8 to 10

300g (1⅓ cups) good quality dark chocolate
300g (1⅓ cups) unsalted butter
300g (1⅓ cups) caster sugar
150g (¾ cup) cocoa powder (not hot chocolate powder)
6 eggs

For the topping:
250g (1 cup) chocolate
100ml (½ cup) cream
25g (¼ stick) butter

- Preheat the oven to 180°C/350°F.
- Start by melting the 300g (1⅓ cups) chocolate and butter together until soft and silky, either in a double boiler or microwave.
- In a separate bowl mix the sugar, eggs and cocoa powder; fold in the buttery chocolate mix and stir until it all comes together.
- Pour into your favourite oiled cake tin. Place this tin into another deep dish, which you will now fill with hot water so that you can bake the cake evenly in a water bath.
- Carefully place this into the oven and bake for 35 to 45 minutes depending on your oven and the thickness of your tins.
- When baked, let the cake rest for a while; often the cake is better the next day.
- You can add any frosting you like but we like to smother this cake with rich dark chocolate ganache and toasted almonds.
- To make the ganache melt together the 250g (1 cup) chocolate and 25g (¼ stick) butter, then stir in the cream. You will notice the consistency change to a thick chocolate goo. Spread this evenly onto the cooled cake and then lick the bowl, spreading chocolate goo all over your face, hair and new top.
- Top the cake with your favourite toasted nuts like almonds, walnuts or hazelnuts, or go mad with some glazed fruits for colour.
- Best served with raspberry sorbet. Yeah!

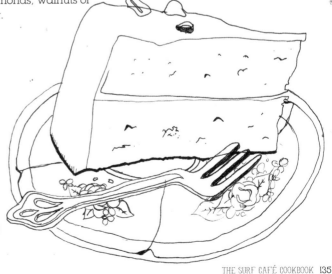

TEA

Barry's or Lyons?!

I never quite appreciated the importance of tea in Ireland until I started travelling and realised that not everyone drinks 10 cups of tea a day! Growing up in our house the kettle was always on. There was always a cup of tea steaming on the table. We spent all our time making tea for my mam and looking forward to the day we would be drinking it ourselves. We weren't really a teapot family for some reason. My best friend in school (and still to this day) Emmajane's house was a different story – teapots all the way. One morning after a regular sleepover in Emmajane's, her dad poured me a cup of tea. As I drank it I nearly choked! It was as thick as tar. His idea of the perfect tea was to make it in a pot and leave it to stew on the hob! So although tea is the most common household item, there are many different ways to make it.

I always laugh looking back when one customer asked me what tea we had. I dutifully listed our selection of herbal teas, the flavours and what they were good for. At the end of my speech, she looked at me and said, "I meant do you use Barry's or Lyons?!" And that's the most definite thing in Ireland, which brand of tea are you, Barry's or Lyons!

HOW DO YOU DRINK YOURS?

"First of all, you have to scald the teapot. Pour in some hot water, swirl it around and then pour it out. Now that your teapot is warm, you're set to put your teabags in along with the hot water you're going to steep them in."
Kira Walton, Voya Seaweed Baths

"Fresh water in the kettle; teabag; stir the bejesus out of it; bit of milk. I'm not really too fussy!"
Fergus McCaffery, forestry consultant and customer

"All standard Irish tea is great. So you have the tea and milk and one sugar. Put the teabag in, leave it for a little while, put the milk in and stir it with the teabag so you can see the colour. The colour is important."
Sinead McGoldrick, former Shells manager

"Barry's tea – obviously! I'm a sucker for marketing."
Barry O'Kane, triathlete and customer

"If you're making tea for two, use a pot and two teabags. Let it sit – as in stew – for two or three minutes. Give it a bit of a stir if you want to make it a bit stronger. Then, this is my mother's tip: always put the milk in the cup before the tea. It mixes the tea and milk better than sticking in a teaspoon and stirring it around."
Jess Smith, organic gardener

WHERE THERE'S TEA THERE'S HOPE

Chocolate Biscuit Cake

Makes 24-30 portions

175g (¾ cup) butter
2 tablespoons golden syrup
250g (1¾ bar) dark chocolate (55-70% cocoa solids)
280g (1 pack) rich tea biscuits
85g (½ cup) raisins
85g (¾ cup) hazelnuts, chopped and roasted

Method

▪ Lightly butter a 23cm (9″ Tin) wsquare cake tin. Combine the butter, syrup and chocolate in a bowl and melt in the microwave, or over a saucepan of gently simmering water.
▪ Whiz the biscuits in a food processor to make coarsely textured crumbs. Alternatively, pop the biscuits into a plastic bag and use a rolling pin.
▪ Stir the crumbs into the melted chocolate mixture and add the raisins and hazelnuts. Mix well. Spoon the mixture into the prepared tin and press down lightly.
▪ Refrigerate until firm and cut into squares to serve.

Shells Café Lemon Squares

Sweet and gooey with a tangy sharp finish. Perfect afternoon treat.

Makes 8 to 10

280g (2¼ cups) plain flour, plus an extra 50g (½ cup)
80g (⅔ cup) icing sugar
1 teaspoon salt
225g (1 cup) unsalted butter
4 free range eggs
350g (1¾ cup) sugar
Juice of four lemons
2 teaspoons lemon zest (TIP: Zest the lemon before you squeeze them!)
1 teaspoon baking powder
Icing sugar to finish

Method

▪ Heat the oven to 170°C/340°F.
▪ Start with the shortbread base. Combine the 280g (2¼ cups) of flour, icing sugar, salt and cold butter in a food processor; mix until crumbly. If you haven't got a food processor, then cut the butter up with two knives. (iIf you use your hands, it would warm the butter and you want to keep it cold.)
▪ Mix just until the dough forms a ball.
▪ Press the dough into a 30x20cm (12″x 8″) baking tin lined with baking paper.
▪ Bake in the oven for 20 to 25 minutes or until golden and set, then leave to cool slightly while you get on with the topping.
▪ Beat the eggs. Add the sugar, lemon juice and lemon zest. In a separate bowl, sift together the remaining 50g (2oz) flour and the baking powder. Add to the egg mixture and stir to combine. Spread onto the cooled shortbread crust and return to the oven for 25 to 30 minutes, or until set.
▪ Cool completely in the tin. Sprinkle with icing sugar and cut into squares. These keep really well, but make sure to store them in an air-tight container. We think they're actually better the next day, as the flavours really develop!

Apple and Donegal Rapeseed Oil Cake

200g (1 cup) golden caster sugar

3 large eggs

150ml (⅔ cup) Donegal rapeseed oil

350g (1¾ cup) flour

½ teaspoon ground ginger

1 teaspoon ground cinnamon

1 teaspoon bicarbonate of soda (bread soda)

1 teaspoon baking powder

110g (⅔ cup) golden raisins or sultanas

80g (⅔ cup) walnuts, crushed

Pinch of salt

Grated zest of a lemon

2 cooking apples, grated

Method

- Preheat the oven 180°C/350°F.
- Place the sultanas or raisins in a bowl of hot water and allow to soak for 15 minutes to plump up.
- Whisk the sugar and eggs until doubled in volume and pale cream in colour. Warm the rapeseed oil and slowly whisk in with the eggs and sugar.
- Sieve the flour, cinnamon, ginger, bread soda, salt and baking powder together. Then gradually add in to the oil and sugar mixture. Fold in well.
- Drain the raisins or sultanas from the water and add to the mixture along with the lemon zest, crushed walnuts and grated apples. Mix thoroughly. The mixture should be stiff at this stage.
- Butter and flour a 20cm spring form cake tin and spoon in the mixture.
- Bake for about 45 minutes until a skewer placed in the middle comes out dry.
- Carefully remove the cake from the tin and allow to cool on a wire rack.

Honey Cream Cheese Frosting

120g (½ cup) cream cheese

2 tablespoons honey

- Whisk together and spread evenly onto the cake once it has cooled.

Easy Scones

Scones are really easy once you get the hang of them. They're a great treat to knock up early in the morning.

Makes 10 scones

900g (7¼ cups) self raising flour
160g (¾ cup) butter, cubed
160g (¾ cup) caster sugar
4 eggs
400ml (1¾ cup) buttermilk
2 tablespoons diced fruit, eg cherries (optional)

Method
- Preheat oven to 180°C/350°F.
- Line a baking tray with baking parchment.
- In a large mixing bowl mix the flour and butter together with your fingers creating a fine grainy texture
- Then work in the sugar.
- In a separate measuring jug combine the eggs and buttermilk. (If you don't have buttermilk add the juice of half a lemon to milk and stir.) Then give the mix a good beating.
- Pour the egg mix into the grainy flour mix and use your hands to bring it all together into a nice sticky dough.
- Do not overwork the dough. This keeps as much air as possible in the mix. In other words, no kneading. If you are using fruit, add it now.
- Turn out onto a well floured surface and pat down to about a two-inch thickness. Cut out round scone shapes with a scone cutter or keep them square and cut out with a sharp knife.
- Place them on the lined baking tray. Leave a bit of space between each one and dust them all with a little flour.
- Pop them in the oven for around 20 to 25 minutes until golden brown.
- Cool on a wire rack.
- Serve with homemade jam and butter or cream.

GET THE LOOK

JANE'S TIPS FOR STYLISH COASTAL LIVING

People always come into the café and rave about the design. We've tried to create the ultimate seafront spot, filled with light, nostalgia, visual interest and comfort. But the thing is, we're not at all precious about it and really keep the emphasis on fun. Cups get broken, the sun ducks behind a cloud, but we just keep rolling. Here are some cheap and easy tips for injecting the sunny seaside into your interior.

Getting the look is an evolution. We never go past a charity shop without heading in for a browse. Quirky little updates along the way keep things looking fresh.

Travel is a great opportunity to buy. You see things with fresh eyes when you're away from home, so follow your instinct in spite of any logistics that might stand in the way. We have an old oil painting of a ship over our coffee machine purchased on a family trip to New Zealand. It cost $3 to buy and then we had to ship it, but it connects us to that place, the people and terrific memories.

Tap into talent. Our "open" sign on the door was knitted by Myles's sister and we have amazing photography that his friend Aniz Duran shot just for us. Waitress Sarah Heath stitched us a garland of bird silhouettes. Don't be afraid to ask your talented friends and relations to contribute. It's a fantastic way to show them off and also lend a sense of personality to your space.

Come up with a plan for collecting. Make it easy to focus by choosing one or two categories to keep an eye out for as you browse in charity shops. You might look out for plates, teapots, tablecloths or souvenir spoons – but if you try to look out for absolutely everything you're likely to find your home overrun (and your bank account empty).

Chop and change. Get a quick fix by periodically swapping out some of your cheaper elements. We use oilcloths on our tables, and when we need a bit of an overhaul we can change these almost instantly.

Revive old furniture. When we opened the café we were on a serious budget, so we needed solutions that were quick, cheap, easy and fun. A bunch of pine chairs were already here but they were so dark they brought the place down. We experimented with refreshing them with oil paint, but this took special equipment and ages to dry. Our solution? We headed to the graffiti supply shop. Compared to a DIY shop, the spray paint we found there was cheaper and came in a broader range of colours. It also dries fast. As the paint wears, it lends a lovely patina.

Mix things up. It's tempting to try to match everything and become a bit insular in your design. Combat this tendency by layering patterns and textures. As long as you keep within a colour scheme, things can still look pulled together.

Less is more. Vintage interiors can feel cluttered, but obviously in a café this isn't really the aesthetic we want. We've set a pared-down Scandinavian backdrop, then used vintage pieces as accents. A blue and white palette, the wooden worktop and horizontal stripes are evidence of the Scandi influence, while flowered tablecloths, mismatched crockery and worn floorboards lend a flavour of days gone by.

Have fun. What one person might call wear and tear, we see as character and cheer. That's why we're more likely to stick an arrangement of wildflowers in a chipped enamel jug than in an anonymous glass vase from the high street.

LOVE
SMILES
JB
CARE

CHRISTMAS

ebrate

tag016

Love from Noddy

special occasions

FOR WHEN YOU REALLY NEED TO PUSH THE BOAT OUT

ST PATRICK'S DAY

Paddy's Day is an all out excuse for a party across Ireland. If you have kids then it's a great day to get out and check out the local parade in Sligo town. Strandhill also does its own parade down the hill to the seafront. Lots of the local kids and adults get involved. All the pubs put on lots of music. Everywhere is buzzing and most people have the day off work, so it can often be an all day session! March is a great time of the year too, as the evenings are getting longer and it's possible to finally get out of winter hibernation.

On Paddy's Day we use lots of green colouring in the café. The icing on the cakes is green and we also serve green cupcakes. We do mint milkshakes too, using mint ice cream. We even did Dr Seuss-inspired green eggs and ham last year, and we couldn't believe the reaction. Apparently everyone's a kid at heart. Lots of people came in wearing red and white striped hats like the Dr Seuss character The Cat in the Hat! The kids loved it, but I think the adults loved it more. It's such a simple dish though – all we did was make up basil oil (page 109), added it to scrambled eggs and served it up with some home baked ham. Et voilà!

IT'S A BIG DAY FOR WEE FOLK

EASTER

As a traditional Catholic country Easter is a pretty big deal in Ireland, second only to Christmas in terms of religious importance. There are public holidays and school holidays to celebrate the rising of Jesus. For non-believers, Easter offers loads of attractions, chocolate, chocolate and more chocolate! It also signifies the end of winter and that summer is on the horizon.

Since we opened Shells, the last few Easters have been hot and sunny, so everyone heads straight to Strandhill for the beach and the surf. There is a caravan site in Strandhill and this reopens that week too, so the population doubles overnight. The village becomes alive once again and is rammed with people. We literally have queues going right out the door over the whole weekend and the patio is packed.

Easter in Shells is about two things – the colour yellow and chocolate! A lot of Easter treats are decorated in yellow icing and gold foil, and of course nearly everything contains chocolate. We love flowers and always try to keep it seasonal. We have a few weeks where daffodils are in abundance and we put them in enamel jugs and place them amongst the Easter treats.

Both of us love to decorate Shells and get into the festivities, so we have egg shaped bunting that we put in the window. (We make this bunting in all different shapes, including hearts and even shamrocks.) It's pretty quick and easy to make. Here's a template and a little how-to – give it a go!

You will need:
- Needle
- Thick thread, or double up a standard thread
- Brightly coloured paper from old books, newspapers or music sheets; be creative with your images. We often collect children's books that are damaged and would otherwise go in the bin. Then we salvage pages with brightly coloured images.

Here's how:
- Trace the egg template and cut out at least 30 egg shapes from your chosen paper. Do more if you want longer bunting.
- Thread the needle, leaving enough thread at each end to make a hook to hang the bunting.
- Then start to sew the eggs in the row, either down the centre or across the top. Make sure to leave about 3cm between each egg, so that they will sit nicely when you hang them.
- In no time at all you'll have your own bunting!
- You can also sew these on a machine, but when you go too fast the needle tends to break going through the paper so be careful.
- This also makes a great gift for the dieter in your life.

HALLOWEEN

Halloween is a great time in Ireland. The evenings are dark and crisp, fires light up everywhere and it's time to start eating to put on that extra layer of fat for winter! As with most countries Halloween is primarily for kids, though most of us adults use it as an excuse to dress up and drink. At Shells we like to host a pumpkin carving party with a prize for the best pumpkin. We serve pumpkin pie and all sorts of pumpkin treats. It's such a laugh and totally different, so here's a quick guide to help you host your own.

▪ Buy in a large number of pumpkins, one per person (with a few extras in case of mistakes).
▪ Have lots of old newspaper to line the table with since pumpkin carving is pretty messy work.
▪ Assign a judge, usually yourself, and don't feel you have to justify your winning choice.
▪ Make sure you have a selection of markers for everyone to outline their drawings on their pumpkins.
▪ Print off some Halloween templates from the internet, a great help to anyone who can't draw.
▪ You'll also need one tea light candle per person and… Lots of beer and wine.
▪ When your friends arrive, tell them to choose a pumpkin, a pen and a stencil if needed.
▪ Talk them through the process of carving, possibly showing a pumpkin you did earlier. Remember you need to cut the top off so you can drop a candle inside and also make sure there are a few oxygen holes at the back to allow the flame to stay lit.
▪ A drill is great for putting oxygen holes in the back. Believe me, everyone loves having a go on the drill.
▪ Award extra points for originality, accuracy and so on.

It's a great night, and we all hit the Strand Bar afterwards with our lit pumpkins. The best thing is driving through the village and seeing all the pumpkins outside people's houses.

CHRISTMAS

Christmas is one of our favourite times of year. Even though it's usually cold and wet, we love it. Shells is buzzing all over Christmas. Our poor baker has some seriously long days as we get major orders for our homemade mince pies, chutneys and jars of red onion marmalade. We even sell mini take home bags of our own Shells coffee. We love giving food as a gift, including a nice food hamper, a box of homemade cookies, delicious wines and mince pies. Believe me, you can never have enough food around Christmas.

We've become known for our homemade Christmas tree and decorations. We have to get creative as we don't have a lot of space in Shells, so we make a paper tree that sits on the wall instead of the floor. It's a bit non-traditional – but then again so is Shells! We make a lot of the extra decorations too. As one of our customers observed, in a café that only serves homemade, why wouldn't you make your own decorations?

So here are a few handy tips to make your own paper tree next year...

▪ The general idea is you outline the shape of a tree on your wall and use different paper cut-outs to fill in the space and create a flat tree.

▪ Get some friends around and serve up some mulled wine while you gossip and cut out shapes.

▪ Decide on the space you have to use. We have a fairly big wall space and the impact is striking – the bigger the better.

▪ Then decide on a colour theme and style. Our first year we went neon, lots of yellow and pinks and we combined this with an animal theme, so we cut out animal shapes, like festive bunnies and doves.

▪ Don't restrict yourself to just paper; try felt, mismatched material, little wool balls – anything and everything.

▪ Then get lots of double-sided stickers to secure the paper. Go to a craft shop and get advice on what to use on your wall surface, so you don't rip off the paint when you remove it all.

▪ If you're worried about the paint, you can create your tree on a large sheet the same colour as the wall surface and stick that up instead.

▪ Then go mad, filling in the space will all your lovingly hand-cut decorations.

▪ Use lots of fairy lights too, it takes the edge off big bright lights and creates a lovely atmosphere.

Another great Christmas idea is to make a chocolate biscuits cake pudding. So instead of the traditional pudding, use the dome shaped mould and follow the recipe on page 139 for the biscuit cake. As it's quite dense in places, make sure you give it enough time to set. Top it with a little fondant icing and edible holly, available from a good baking shop.

HOW TO MAKE A
SHELLS GIFT BAG

Can be made to suit and a different shape or sized gift (whether it be odd or evenly shaped). Make it as personal as possible and it can be used again and again! by Sarah Heath

fig 1
The first taste of a present is its presentation!

fig 2
What's needed:
1. Template (for this gift size I used a simple a4 sheet of paper).
2. Scissors (sharp as possible).
3. Pins.
4. Rope or ribbon.
5. Needle and thread (similar or contrasting colour to fabric).
6. Fabric. Whatever kind you like! dependent on the amount of bags you would like to make, it's up to you. safe is twice the length and width of your template.
7. Fabric paint (for personal touches).

fig 3
Template cutting: place template on fabric and pin together.

fig 4
Note: make sure you have two sides of fabric.

fig 5
To make the draw string top, measure an inch and a half to 2 inches and fold outwards on both sides and pin.

fig 6
Pin together both pieces of fabric approx half an inch all around the rim of the bag.

fig 7
Sew the bottom and each side of the bag by hand or sewing machine if available.

fig 8
Turn the bag inside out (the right way around!).

fig 9
You will be left with two gaps on each side of the draw string openings. Put a couple of stitches in one side at the very top, allowing space for rope or ribbon still to be fed through.

fig 10
Put a pin through the end of your draw string.

fig 11
Push the pin through the hole and feed it around the top of the bag.

fig 12
Make sure it comes out even at each side and knot both sides to prevent the draw string from going back into the bag.

fig 13
Paint or stitch a personal message or image; or free hand cut stencil for repeated imagery.

fig 14
And there you have it, use these bags as a first reflection of your gift or use them for storage for your own little knick knacks.

Enjoy :)

soul food

After dark, feed your soul with warm and comforting food.

Thai Pumpkin Broth

Serves 4 to 6

1 medium pumpkin, peeled and chopped

1 large onion, peeled and diced

2 cloves garlic, peeled and finely chopped

1 tablespoon fresh ginger, grated

2 red chillies, thinly sliced (deseeded for no heat, or leave seeds in for more heat)

1 tin coconut milk

1 zest and juice of a fresh lime

1 dash olive or seasme oil

1 drizzle honey

1 litre (4¼ cups) chicken or vegetable stock

Handful of fresh corriander

- Preheat oven to 200°C/400°F. Roast the chopped pumpkin with a dash of olive oil and a drizzle of honey and season with salt and pepper. Roast for about 25 minutes, stirring occasionally.
- In a hot, thick bottomed pot, sweat down the garlic, onions and ginger in sesame or olive oil until they are nice and golden. Add in 1 litre of chicken or vegetable stock. Next add in the roasted pumpkin with the juices. Boil and stir for 20 minutes.
- Take it off the boil and add the chillies, coconut milk, lime zest and juice. Season to taste.
- Dish up and garnish with lots of fresh coriander. Serve with a thick slice of brown soda bread.

PS You can turn this into a main meal by adding grilled chicken strips, green beans and noodles!

Lamb Stew

When you think of Irish cuisine, the first thing that comes to mind is Irish lamb stew. It's a very basic simple flavour, so using the best quality ingredients if very important.

Serves 4 to 6

900g (2lb) diced lamb
6 large carrots
9 medium potatoes
2 small onions, diced
800ml (3⅔ cups) of good stock
Thyme
Parsley
Drizzle of oil

Method

- Make the stock before you start with the stew. If you haven't got time, a good beef stock cube will work just as well.
- Peel and chop the vegetables, but make sure to keep them chunky.
- Dice the onion. Drizzle some oil into a hot casserole dish and sauté the onions to a nice soft golden stage.
- Throw in the diced lamb and brown evenly, keeping the heat on high.
- Throw in the vegetables and a few sprigs of thyme, then sweat the vegetables for around five minutes before adding the stock.
- Let the stew simmer on low heat with the lid on for around two hours, slowly blip blopping away.
- Take off the lid and spoon out some of the potato into a bowl and mash it up with a fork. Return it to the dish. This is how the Irish stew gets its character – lots of small white potato bits with meat and potato.
- Before serving, throw in a handful of chopped parsley. Season with salt and pepper. Serve with chunky warm bread.

TIP: Some Irish stews have pearl barley in them. If you want to use pearl barley, add two tablespoons of barley with the vegetables, but add a third more stock.

Chuck & Blade Fore rib Sirloin Rump Topside

Silverside

Neck

Thick flank

Thin rib

Clod Thick rib

Flank

Brisket Leg

Shin

CHOOSING GOOD MEAT

Butchers are a great source for information and services that people don't utilise enough. Introduce yourself to your local butcher and then drop some serious cash on his meat, right before a big dinner party for example. You'll certainly grab his attention and he'll look out for you in the future.

Ask about different cuts of meat, ask about good bargains like beef shin or pork belly and ask his recommendations on how to cook what you buy. Find out how long he hangs his meat for and whether he specialises in dry aged or home cured products. Does he make his own sausages? Does he cure his own bacon? Which farm does it come from, and is it local?

A good butcher should be able to pre order any meat specialities, including odder cuts like beef cheeks or ox tail. Many now carry local farmers' fresh eggs. In some places it's possible to bring your knives in to your butcher to get them sharpened. Obviously don't do this during a lunchtime rush, but visit instead in the early morning trading times.

Finally give your butcher feedback, good or bad. Be honest and open; perhaps he's trying a new farm and their products taste fantastic or maybe the new apprentice is not cutting well. And when you're satisfied tell others. A good butcher is a busy butcher.

Beef 'n' Mushroom
with anchovy butter

Don't like anchovies!? This butter will change that view very
quickly. It's a perfect compliment to this dish - quick, easy and
so tasty.

Serves 2

400g (1 lb) rump or sirloin steak, cut into thin strips and marinated in oil, garlic and red wine
4 large portobello mushrooms, thinly sliced (oyster or shitake mushrooms are also fine)
2 streaky bacon rashers, sliced into sticks
Bunch flat leaf parsley, chopped
1 garlic clove, diced
Salt and pepper
Knob of butter (¼ stick)
Splash of oil
2 slices hot buttered toast
Handful mixed baby leaves
2 slices of anchovy butter

• Start by cutting your favourite steak into nice stir-fry strips and let them
marinate for a while in some oil, garlic and red wine.
• In a hot pan, splash in some oil and a knob of butter. Pop in the diced
garlic and stir around. Now add the bacon and mushrooms and toss
around until the mushrooms begin to soften. (Adding a splash of water to
help steam the mushrooms will help them cook.) Set aside in a bowl.
• Reheat the pan till it's nice and hot and almost smoking, then toss in the
beef strips. Stir-fry for about three to five minutes on a high heat. In the last
minute pop in the bread to be toasted. About this time, toss the mushroom
mix into the beef and add the chopped parsley. If it's a little dry add a knob
of butter.
• Once cooked to your liking, place the mix on top of the buttered toast
and finish with a knob of anchovy butter. This should start to melt over the
mushrooms. Sprinkle mixed baby leaves on top. Allow to rest for a minute
so the juices start running.
• Tuck in and enjoy!

Flavoured Butters

Adding different herbs and
flavours to butter can greatly
enhance a dish. Our personal
favourite is Anchovy butter, which
is especially on a good steak with
mushrooms. The butter doesn't
taste like anchovies but gives
the steak a whole new dimension.
Flavoured butter is easy to make
and a great way to experiment.
Plus it freezes well too.

You will need a 425g (**2 cups**) block of
butter at room temperature that's soft
to the touch.
Add the options below to the butter
and blend with a hand blender.

Anchovy Butter
1 tin anchovies, chopped (8 to 10 fillets)
2 teaspoons chopped parsley

Seaweed Butter
2 tablespoon chopped dillisk seaweed
Zest of lemon
Pinch of salt

Sage, Rocket, Dill or Basil Butter
3 tablespoons herbs, finely chopped
Add the zest of a lemon if you like

Tomato Basil Butter
2 tablespoons tomato puree
5 basil leaves, chopped
Splash of balsamic vinegar

Garlic Butter
4 cloves garlic, finely diced
2 teaspoons chopped parsley

How to store flavoured butter
• Spoon out the soft flavoured butter
onto a long piece of cling film.
• Fold over the cling film and gently
shape the butter into a sausage-like
form inside the cling film.
• Pick up the cling-filmed butter from
either end and roll and twist the ends
to form a sausage-like casing.
• Tie off the ends and refrigerate
or freeze.

Baby Lamb Chops
with Yummy Spiced Spinach and Potatoes

There's no shortage of spuds or lamb in Ireland. This is a beautiful dish that showcases the amazing food that can be produced from food literally on our doorstep. Interestingly, it's also a new take on the Indian dish saag aloo. The potato and spinach part also makes a great side dish, or throw a poached egg on top and you have an awesome brunch.

Serves 4

450g (1 lb) new potatoes

350g (11½ cups) spinach, without stems

2 tablespoon rapeseed oil (we use Donegal oil)

1 onion, thinly sliced

1 garlic clove, finely chopped

1 red chilli, deseeded and finely chopped

1 teaspoon freshly grated ginger

2 teaspoons garam masala

1 teaspoon coriander seed

1 teaspoon fennel seed

2-3 tablespoons double cream

Sea salt and freshly ground pepper

1 teaspoon ground cumin

8 small lamb chops

- Preheat the grill on high.
- Chop the potatoes into quarters, keeping them the same size. Put into a saucepan, cover with water, add salt and bring to the boil. Simmer for about 10 minutes, until tender. Drain.
- Wash the spinach (don't worry about drying it, leave a splash of water on the leaves) and place into a saucepan. Cover and place over a medium heat until the spinach has wilted in its own liquid. This should only take a few minutes. Drain and leave until cool, then use your hands to squeeze out as much liquid as you can. Chop the spinach roughly.
- Heat the oil in a frying pan and add the coriander and fennel seeds.
- Gently sweat the onion for about 10 minutes or until soft. Add the garlic, chilli, ginger and garam masala. Cook for a couple of minutes more, then add the cooked potatoes into the pan. Cook for a couple of minutes.
- While this is cooking, season the chops with a little oil, salt, pepper and ground cumin. Then place under the grill, two to three minutes on each side, depending on the thickness. I love it when the fat goes nice and crispy!
- Now add the chopped spinach to the pan with the potatoes and cook briefly just to warm through. At this point add in the double cream for extra richness and season with salt and pepper. Now serve alongside the chops.

Campervan Casserole

This is a great one-pot wonder. Bang it all together and all you need is one large pot and one gas ring! There's minimal washing up too...

Serves 4

4 chicken thighs

4 chicken drumsticks

2 cooked chorizo sausages, chopped

1 chopped onion

4 chopped cloves garlic

½ glass red wine

2 tins chopped tomatoes

2 tins butter beans or cannellini beans

Tablespoon sugar

Splash or a tablespoon red wine vinegar

3 dashes Worcestershire sauce

Drizzle of olive oil

Salt and pepper

½ teaspoon paprika (smoked paprika is great if you can find it, but use slightly less as it's quite fiery)

½ teaspoon cayenne (optional)

2 tablespoon chopped rosemary

Zest of one lemon

Chopped parsley to garnish

- Heat up a large casserole dish and add a drizzle of olive oil.
- Throw in the chopped garlic, onion and rosemary. Sauté the onions for a couple of minutes then add the chopped chorizo sausage. Cook and stir for two minutes.
- Add in the chicken, placing it skin down on the sizzle to brown the skin. Cook for another five minutes, stirring once halfway to turn the chicken.
- Then add the beans, tinned tomato, red wine, vinegar and paprika. If you like it spicy, add in the cayenne now.
- Stir around and add the sugar, salt and pepper and Worcestershire sauce.
- Reduce the heat and allow to simmer on a low heat for a good two hours, low and slow, giving it the occasional stir.
- Turn off the heat and let it rest for another 10 minutes before serving. Grate on some lemon zest just before you dish up. Sprinkle some chopped parsley on each serving.
- Great with thick cut bread; a cheap and cheerful dish with lots of flavour!

POTATOES!

There are few Irish households where the potato isn't a staple, and anyone who makes even a basic stab at growing vegetables will plant a few spuds in their garden.

They are eaten boiled, mashed, fried, chipped and baked, mixed with cabbage or scallions to make colcannon or champ, made into potato cakes and used to top pies and to thicken soups or stews. It's common to find potatoes cooked two different ways on the same dinner plate.

Irish people are very particular about their potatoes. Typically a supermarket will stock at least five or six different varieties, often many more, with the varieties changing depending on the season and each suited to a particular method of cooking.

Of all foods, the humble spud is certainly the most traditional. We may not be dependent on them in the way we were in the past but there are a lot of Irish people for whom a dinner without potatoes is not a dinner at all.

Mashed Potato

Did you know that there are over 100 varieties of potato, each with its own distinctive character? In Ireland the Irish LOVE potatoes, especially mashed. There are loads of variations of mashed potato. Here's our definitive guide to the best mash.

Serves 4 to 5

900g (2 lb) potato (Kerr's pink are the best), peeled and chopped into pieces of the same size
300ml (1¼ cups) creamy milk
50g (¼ cup) butter
Salt and freshly ground pepper
1 organic egg yolk (optional)

- Place the potatoes into a saucepan of cold water, add a good pinch of salt and bring to the boil.
- When the potatoes are half cooked, around 15 minutes into cooking, strain off two-thirds of the water, replace the lid on the saucepan, put onto a gentle heat and allow the potatoes to steam until they're cooked.
- Mash the potato while hot.
- Bring the milk to the boil, and add the boiling creamy milk to the hot mashed potatoes; mix to get a soft light consistency. If you're using eggs, add them now and then beat in the butter. (For the butter, 50g (¼ cup) will make quite a rich mash; you can use less butter if you prefer).

TIP: You must add the milk while it's boiling, otherwise the potato will go lumpy and gluey. Never use a hand blender – use a masher, whisk or fork instead!

- Season with salt and freshly ground pepper. Taste and add more butter and seasoning if necessary.

You can reheat potatoes (in the oven only) – just make sure to cover with foil while reheating so it doesn't form a skin.

Variations:

Scallion Champ or Mash

110g (1 cup) scallions (spring onions), chopped
Follow the main recipe. While the mash is hot, mix the spring onions and boiling milk, and beat in the butter. Season with salt and pepper.

Wild Garlic Mash

Follow the main recipe, but add 50 to 75g (¾ - 1¼ cup) roughly chopped wild garlic leaves to the milk just as it comes to the boil.

Mustard Mash

Follow the main recipe, but add two tablespoons Dijon mustard along with the butter.

Colcannon

This is a strong traditional Irish dish. In the past kale would have been used, but now cabbage is more common. This is a great comfort food dish and is making a major comeback!

900g (2 lb) old potatoes
450g (6½ cups) savoy or spring cabbage
50g (¼ cup) butter
250ml (1 cup) milk
25g (¼ cup) spring onion
Salt and pepper

- Place the potatoes into a saucepan of cold water, add a good pinch of salt and bring to the boil.
- When the potatoes are half cooked, around 15 minutes into cooking, strain off two-thirds of the water, replace the lid on the saucepan, put onto a gentle heat and allow the potatoes to steam until they're tender.
- Remove the dark outer leaves from the cabbage. Wash the rest and cut into quarters, removing the core. Cut the cabbage finely across the grain. Boil in a little boiling water until soft. Drain and season with salt, pepper and a little butter.
- When the potatoes are just cooked, put the milk and spring onion into a saucepan and bring to the boil. Mash the potatoes while they are still warm, beating in enough boiling milk to make a fluffy puree.
- Then stir in the cooked cabbage and taste for seasoning.
- For perfection, serve in a hot dish with a lump of butter melting in the centre. Sprinkle a parsley leaf or two on top for that added special touch.

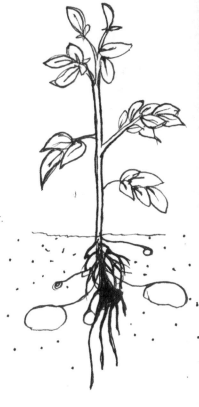

Vegetable Gratin with Durrus Cheese

A big phat veggie dish with great colours
and flavours. The gratin can be made in
advance too, so you're not stressing if
you have all your mates around. Serve it
with a nice green garden salad and mustard
vinaigrette. Durrus cheese is a good strong
semi soft cheese from West Cork that melts
deliciously well. Any other semi soft cheese
will also have this affect.

Serves 8

4 medium potatoes

½ celeriac

1 small white onion

4 cloves of garlic

2 carrots

2 beetroot

300ml (1½ cups) cream

30g (¼ stick) butter

Salt and pepper

Durrus cheese, sliced, enough to cover the top of the gratin

- Preheat the oven to 180°C/350°F.
- Prep all the veg by peeling and thinly slicing using a mandolin or a sharp knife. You want nice thin discs of vegetable, a bit like crisps!
- In a large oven-proof dish, rub a small clove of garlic onto the surface and follow suit with the butter.
- Layer the vegetables in order – first the potato, then the celeriac, scatter some garlic and onions, then the carrots and last the beetroot. This will give an amazing array of colours in each slice of gratin.
- Next pour in the cream and squish down with a spatula to pack it all in.
- Pop it in the oven and bake for around 40 minutes. Take it out and poke it with a knife; if it's 'al dente' (semi soft) it's ready for the cheese.
- Cover as much as possible with slices of semi soft cheese. Pop back in the oven for a further 20 minutes until it is all cooked, crispy and bubbly!
- Allow to rest for five minutes or so, and then slice a nice big square onto a plate using a spatula.
- Serve with a baby leaf salad and some salsa (see page 117).

Perfect Bangers and Mash

Such a simple dish, but hard to get right. Make sure you follow all the steps for the ideal meal.

You need four great things to come together for a good bangers and mash:

- Good award-winning sausage. Choose ones that are fresh and plump from a butcher over those from a supermarket.
- Perfect Mashed Potato (see page 161)
- Proper homemade gravy, not from a packet. You want deep, full flavour, and that's the hardest part.
- Sweet, dark and sticky caramelised onions, and lots of them.

Gravy

Serves 4

3 onions

1.5kg (3.3 lb) butchers' bones and offcuts

2 carrots, chopped

4 tomatoes, crushed

2 heads of garlic

Woody herbs, including thyme, rosemary or sage

200ml (¾ cup) red wine

Worcestershire sauce or soy sauce

1 heaped teaspoon cornflour

1 tablespoon sugar or berry jam

1 tablespoon Bovril (optional)

Splash of oil

Cup of hot water.

Salt and crushed black pepper

- With the real gravy, it's a long process but worth it. In a large baking tray, quarter the onions, then throw in the bones, scraps of meat, chopped carrots, tomatoes, a head of garlic and your favourite herbs. Drizzle with lots of oil and add a cup of red wine. Roast on a high heat at around 200°C/392°F for about 45 minutes, stirring halfway through.
- After 45 minutes take the tray out of the oven and give everything a good hard stir. Take out the bones, woody herbs and anything else which is not edible such as onion skin and garlic skin.
- Mash the rest with a fork, scraping the bottom of the roasting tin to capture the meat dripping bits. Next place the tray on a hot hob. Add a cup of hot water, a splash of soy or Worcester sauce, a tablespoon of sugar or berry jam, two pinches of salt, cracked black pepper and if you have it a tablespoon of Bovril.
- Bring to the boil and reduce to a nice consistency. This should take 10 to 15 minutes, while you stir, scrape and mash with a fork to keep breaking everything up. If it's too thin you might have to add a teaspoon of cornflour (but mix it into a paste first with a splash of water).
Gravy done!

Sausages

Makes 8 sausages (2 per person)

- Grill sausages nice and slowly in the oven, 170°C/340°F. Remember to turn them for even colour. Alternatively you can boil them in a shallow pot of water for about 10 minutes. Then for some colour, finish them off in a hot pan with a drizzle of oil.

Caramelised onions

6 onions, sliced

- Find the thickest pan or pot, the heavier the better. Heat it up with a splash of oil and get it hot hot!
- Throw in the sliced onions, and listen for the swish of the hot pan.
- Stir the onions around so they get coated in oil and leave them for about five minutes. Do not stir them again.
- The onions should be sizzling away. With a wooden spoon or a spatula, scrape the bottom of the pot giving the onions a good stir.
- You will notice a nice sticky brown layer forming on the bottom; this is the good stuff. Scrape and stir into the onions... Wait... And continue to do this for at least another 30 minutes, until the onions are a dark brown colour, sticky and sweet. Yum...

THE CRAIC

McGARRIGLES

I remember walking around Sligo one day and seeing this quirky little pub. It had one wall of bold floral wallpaper with mismatched pictures all over it and then an array of vintage light fittings. It was love at first sight! I had to go in. I was so relieved to find a cool, different and interesting place. It was a bit of reassurance that the west of Ireland didn't have to be just about rural life, green hills and Guinness!

It was the first pub in town that became my little regular spot. What I didn't realise at the time was that Tricky had just taken it over a few months previously. So we found ourselves on a similar journey, both starting to run our own businesses and trying to do something different in Sligo.

As Myles and I always work weekends and they are our busiest time, we tend to wind down on a Monday and Tuesday night. So we rocked up in Tricky's one Monday, not expecting too much – and I was blown away. There was a cool band playing in front of the fire; picture lots of long hair, beards and mandolins! They were playing a mix of bluegrass and folk music and the atmosphere was amazing. Also the crowd was diverse, like anyone and everyone was in there and all ages too. It's the kind of place I bring my parents to as well as my friends. There are not many places that can achieve that balance.

Then during Culture Week in Sligo I went upstairs in Tricky's to the venue part of the pub and didn't quite know what to expect. There was the most amazing circus act on. Totally different and unexpected and that's what I like about it. You never quite know what's going to be happening when you pop into Tricky's, but it's always cutting-edge and ahead of the crowd.

One great thing as well is that we help each other out. We've done a little bit of music in Shells and Tricky is always there lending an amp or offering advice on the best speakers. It's priceless to know you have a few people to turn to if you ever get stuck, and Tricky is definitely one of them.

Tricky Caheny, publican (opposite)

"My family have had a bar in Sligo since 1890. My great-grandfather set it up originally. Then my grandfather – who I'm named after – ran it for a good few years with two of his brothers. My parents gave it a whole new lease of life in the Seventies.

About 15 years ago my parents divorced. They decided that instead of selling any assets because it was in the family for so long it would be better if my mother stayed on and ran it until either me or my brother Paul were of an age to take it on as an inheritance. My brother is a great academic and never really got into bar work. It was something that I fell into as a round peg in a round hole.

About two years ago I wanted to open something of my own rather than sitting back in something my parents had created. So after many years experience and great tuition from my mother I decided to take on McGarrigles.

We've got a very vibrant live music scene that really is on the edge rather than anything mainstream. We never have cover bands; we always try to give fresh new artists as much scope as possible to play. It's a very bohemian atmosphere, lots of interesting characters coming in, a lot of different, quirky, really new music that's breaking out. It's definitely the ethos of the place to constantly push things forward."

Guinness

In 1759 Arthur Guinness signed a 9,000-year lease on a disused brewery at St James's Gate in Dublin and began brewing porter and ale. Forty years later he opted to abandon ale and focus on his increasingly popular porter. Not a bad decision, as it happens. This simple recipe of roasted malted barley, hops, yeast and water is now enjoyed around the world and is the hands-down favourite drink of Ireland. Over 10 million glasses of Guinness are enjoyed every single day, and 1.8 billion pints are sold annually.

The two-part pour
Should you find yourself behind the bar in an Irish pub, the first thing you'll need to master is how to prepare the perfect pint. Guinness requires the famous "two-part pour". Start with a clean, dry glass. Tilt the glass at 45 degrees, and fill with draught Guinness until it's three-quarters full. Allow the surge to settle, and only then should you fill the glass completely to the top.

Home brew
If you're at home, there's a reasonable chance you won't be drinking your Guinness out of a barrel. Here's the method for achieving a perfect pour anyway. First let your cans chill for no less than three hours. Take out a clean, dry glass. Now pour the contents of a can into your glass in a single smooth action.

The Black Velvet
This drink was in fact born in London following the death of Queen Victoria's beloved husband Albert. Everyone was grieving when a bar steward allegedly decided that champagne should go into mourning too and so he added Guinness to the bubbly. To make your own, halfway fill a champagne flute with Guinness, then slowly top it up with chilled champagne.

THE CONNOISSEURS' APPROACH TO GETTING A
GOOD GUINNESS
• First of all, ask a local where to get
the best Guinness.
• A Guinness must rest for a few minutes;
never drink it straight away.
• The first sip should be generous, so
make sure the head covers your lip.
• Never add blackcurrant, no matter how
tempting it sounds!
• Get the next pint of Guinness when the first
one is three-quarters finished to ensure the
next pint is well rested before you're ready
to tuck in.
• Chase the Guinness with a fresh oyster, shot
of whiskey and then on to another Guinness!

Guinness and Beef Stew

Guinness, Ireland's famous black stout, has been brewed in Dublin since 1759. Back in the day it was treated as food. They used to call the pint the 'liquid food'.

Nowadays the 'liquid food' is used increasingly in cooking. It's a tasty addition to stews and casseroles, helping to tenderize the meat and imparting its distinctive malty flavour to any dish. This recipe makes a wonderful gutsy stew which tastes even better a day or two after it is made.

Serves 4 to 6

900g (2 lb) lean stewing beef
3 tablespoons oil
2 tablespoons flour
Salt and a large heaping of cracked black pepper
2 large onions, coarsely chopped
5 small shallots, peeled but kept whole
1 bay leaf
1 large clove garlic, crushed (optional)
2 tablespoons tomato puree, dissolved in 4 tablespoons water
250ml (1¼ cups) Guinness
2 cups carrots, cut into chunks
1 cup of parsnips, cut into chunks
Sprig of thyme
Parsley to serve

Method

- Trim the meat of any fat or gristle, cut into cubes of two inches (5cm) and toss them in a bowl with one tablespoon oil.
- Season the flour with salt and freshly cracked pepper.
- Toss the meat in the flour mixture.
- Heat the remaining oil in a wide frying pan over a high heat.
- Brown the meat on all sides.
- Add the onions, shallots, bay leaf, crushed garlic to the pan, cover and cook gently for about five minutes.
- Transfer the contents of the pan to a casserole, and pour some of the Guinness into the frying pan.
- Bring to a boil and stir to dissolve the caramelized meat juices on the pan.
- While the Guinness is boiling add the tomato puree into the casserole dish with the meat.
- Then pour the Guinness mix onto the meat with the remaining Guinness; add the carrots, parsnips and the thyme. Stir, taste, and add a little more salt if necessary.
- Cover with the lid of the casserole and simmer very gently until the meat is tender, two to three hours. The stew may be cooked on top of the stove or in a low oven at 150°C/300°F.
- Taste and correct the seasoning. Scatter with lots of chopped parsley.
- Serve with your fave mashed potato (see page 161).

HOW TO CHOOSE A GOOD WINE

Here are a few tips for selecting that perfect bottle of wine.

1. Find a friendly independent wine merchant who will take the time to get to know your preferred nuances when it comes to style, region and grape variety.

2. You get what you pay for. Spending marginally more on your bottle will open up the range and improve the quality and your enjoyment considerably.

3. Consider the story behind the label and the heritage of the wine. Small boutique wineries are often family run. Find out about their traditions and how their location has influenced the character of the wine from climate through to terroir.

4. Don't be afraid to 'drink' outside the box. There are over 250,000 different grape varieties worldwide, and most of us have only experienced a few of these. With many wineries exploring the more funky varietals, your wine merchant will be able to introduce you to some interesting new kids on the block including Godello, Garnacha, Verdelho and Bobal.

5. TLC: handle your bottle with a little love and understanding to allow the wine to deliver. Take the time to chill your whites well and pop open your reds in advance to allow them to breathe. Speak to a wine merchant who can help you with sourcing the perfect wine glass too. It all helps.

6. What's on the menu? Food aficionados will take great care and detail to source the finest quality fare. Adopt the same approach to your wine selection and consider your menu; the perfect match really can make the meal.

7. When you find a wine you like, make a note of it.

8. When you're shopping in a supermarket, explore the wines that are normally out of your price bracket but currently on offer. Broaden your horizons further by joining a local wine club through a wine merchant.
– *Wine expert, Jenny Morgan*

TRIED AND TESTED

The wines we have chosen for Shells are the classics with slight twists. We always look for a balance between really good wine, great character but with affordability.

We have a classic french style Sauvignon Blanc. It's from the Loire Valley. We went with a French one as everything in the shops these days seems to be from New Zealand. Sometimes European whites seem a bit more complicated and harder to find the right one. We certainly did a lot of tastings to find this beauty!

Our house white is is a very drinkable Pinot Grigio. It's light, crisp and works well with a lot of our lunch time dishes.

Our stellar wine is a honey coloured Chardonnay. This is a new style Chardonnay, that hasn't been aged in an oak barrel, so therefore it doesn't have the traditional oaky flavour. It's creamy and smooth and goes really well with spicy food.

We have some real gems in our reds too. Our house red is a French Cabernet Savignon. This is light and fruity and a lovely light lunchtime wine. If you prefer something with a bit more punch we have a fantastic Australian Shiraz. it has a long herb and peppery finish. A lot of our customers have been converted to Shiraz because of it.

The sister wine to our Chardonnay is our Malbec. A classic Argentinian wine, Malbecs are being seen more and more on menus. It's fast becoming the new red to drink. It's got loads of character and great depth.

For a special occasion, or for Sunday brunch we do a great organic Prosescco by the glass, it's light, dry and full of bubbles. We have gorgeous edible hibiscus flowers that we add to a glass to make it a 'Pink Prosecco'- perfect after a spring surf!

THE CLASSIC IRISH CHEESE BOARD

For any cheese lover, the idea of being able to work your way round a selection of cheeses is one of the best ways of indulging your passion. When you put together a cheese board, aim for a contrast of textures, tastes and shapes. Mild to strong, rounds and wedges, light against dark, soft and hard – it's about making it look good as well as taste good.

A classic cheese board will contain a cheese from one of each of the main styles. Leave out any you don't like, but I always like to throw on a wild card which I think people won't have eaten before. It's always nice to surprise guests and introduce them to something new.

Top choices and the ones we regularly use in Shells are:
- **Soft Goats Cheese:** From Bluebell Falls, produced on the Keane family farm in County Clare. They only use goats' milk from within their farm and produce a rich creamy cheese.
- **Crozier Blue:** Medium-strength blue cheese with a creamy texture. Made in Ireland, this is one of the country's few blue cheeses. It's made from sheep's milk on the farm of Jane and Louis Grubb by their daughter Sarah Furno.
- **Durrus Farmhouse Cheese:** This deeply flavoured, coral-coloured, semi-soft rind washed cheese is made from the milk of local West Cork herds.
- **Classic Irish Cheddar, Mount Callan:** A hard cheese made only during the summer months by Micheal and Lucy Hayes using traditional rennet and raw milk from their own herd of Montbelliard cows on the family farm in North Clare.

I always serve my cheeseboard with an abundance of seasonal fruits and chutneys as well as fresh rocket and oat crackers. All-time favorites are fresh strawberries, cherries, grapes, sliced pear and apple. Apple, peach and tomato chutneys always go down well with cheese.

If you need some inspiration I feel the best and most dedicated cheesemongers in Ireland are Sheridans Cheesemongers. They are both retailers and wholesalers of quality Irish and other European foods, sourcing excellent quality artisan products and where possible forging links directly with the food producers themselves. Every time I go to Sheridans I always come out with a bag full of goodies and wheels of cheese I hadn't tasted before!

Here in Sligo we have a great cheese supplier who hauls an amazing variety of cheeses to the Farmers Market in the Sligo IT every Saturday morning.

CREENY

A rich sweet luxurious taste. Deep sharp tangy, as it ages it almost takes your breathe away!

· SHEEP MILK
UNPASTEURISED
VEGETARIAN RENNET
BELTURBET, CO.CAVAN

€36.00
price per kilo

WHISKEY

Let's be honest: there's only so much Guinness you can drink. After a few pints you might feel it's time to move on. This is where whiskey enters the scene. The most popular Irish whiskeys include Jamesons, Midleton and Powers. Odd as it might seem, we've found airport shops can be a good place to browse the producers both large and small. Plenty of people drink Irish whiskey neat and some have it over ice, but adding a drop of water is the way to go if you want to fully release the flavours.

IRISH WHISKEY:
FAST FACTS

• Ireland is reputed to be where whiskey was invented.

• John Jameson, master distiller and creator of one of Ireland's best known whiskeys, was born in Scotland.

• Legally Irish Whiskey must be matured on the island of Ireland for no fewer than three years.

THE BABY POWER

GUARANTEED OVER SEVEN YEARS OLD

GUARANTEED PURE POT STILL

Homemade Baileys!

Every time we make this our friends just can't believe it. They are so impressed, and what they don't know is just how easy it is to make. Often associated with winter, I think it is a great summer eve's drink for winding down from a day of action, either in the water or on the beach. Kick back after dinner with this fresh Baileys and enjoy a late sunset!

225 ml (1 cup) Irish whiskey
1 can sweetened condensed milk
450ml (2 cups) double cream
2 tablespoons liquid chocolate
½ tablespoon almond extract
1 teaspoon vanilla extract
4 eggs
1 teaspoon instant coffee

- Mix all ingredients in blender.
- Chill well before serving. Serve over ice. Can substitute milk for double cream. Add more or less whiskey, to taste.
- Blend and refrigerate.

This recipe should be kept refrigerated and shaken well before serving if it has been allowed to sit for a while. You should also be aware that because of the eggs, it only stays fresh for a few days.

After Dinner Drink: Irish Mist

Myles is a serious after dinner drink person. When we lived in South Africa a meal was was always finished with a digestif or a sticky sweet dessert wine. Same in France, where there's nothing better to warm you up than a sip of *eau de vie*. Since moving to Ireland, Myles has become a bit of a whiskey expert and his favourite and only after dinner drink is an Irish Mist! A bit of an old school drink, Irish Mist was actually the first liqueur to be produced in Ireland when commercial production began in 1947 at Tullamore. It's best on the rocks but if you can't handle it straight it's delish with lime and coke.

Baileys
If you don't fancy dessert but want something creamy, then it has to be a double Baileys on ice. I always ask for some fresh chocolate flakes on top. It's the best of both worlds: chocolatey and alcoholic.

JULES / STONE SOUP

Irish Coffee

50ml (¼ cup) Irish whiskey
200ml (1 cup) coffee
50ml (¼ cup) double cream
Brown sugar

This is a cocktail consisting of hot coffee, Irish whiskey and sugar, stirred and topped with thick cream. The coffee is drunk through the cream. The original recipe explicitly uses cream that has not been whipped, although whipped cream is often used. Sugar should be brown and not white.

Black coffee is poured into a long glass with a handle. Next add two measures of Irish whiskey and at least one level teaspoon of sugar, stirring it in until fully dissolved. The sugar is essential for floating liquid cream on top. Thick cream is carefully poured over the back of a spoon initially held just above the surface of the coffee and gradually raised a little. The layer of cream will float on the coffee without mixing.

SUPPER CLUBS

We've been overwhelmed with the popularity of our supper clubs. Almost as soon as a new one is announced it gets booked up. But you don't have to have a café to host a successful one of these modern-day dinner parties with a twist. Follow our simple guidelines to transform your own dining table into a thriving supper club of your own.

Limit the numbers. You don't want to be overwhelmed in the kitchen, so eight people is the ideal length for a guest list. And anyway, if you invite more than that you may find yourself crossing the county to collect enough chairs for everyone!

Set out the plan. Some supper clubs are like book clubs; you decide on a group of people and these members meet up once a month. Or you can keep it more fluid; your supper club might have a shifting guest list. If you go for this option, try to invite a new mix of people each time.

Determine any dietary requirements. Before you get too carried away with planning, be sure to find out what your guests can and can't eat.

Write out your menu. Start with how many people you're going to feed, then choose dishes based on that. Don't try to copy someone else's style; the menu should ideally feature your own personality.

Cook what you're comfortable with. If you venture too far beyond your comfort zone, the stress comes out in the cooking. It's better to serve something simple but beautifully made than an overcomplicated dish that's really outside of your abilities.

Do as much advance prep as possible. Choose dishes that won't keep you slaving over a hot stove and away from your guests, such as a fabulous roast. The more

organised you can be, the more you'll be able to enjoy the party.

Broaden the horizons with one new veg. Try to introduce a seasonal vegetable that most people would never eat, like Jerusalem artichoke, celeriac or kohlrabi. If you buy it at your local market, ask the vendor their best tips for preparation.

Emphasise interactivity. If you can get your guests participating in some aspect of preparation of the meal, it gets people bonding with each other and also with your theme. Extend the interaction into eating too; food that gets you involved around the table facilitates new friendships.

Educate and inspire. A supper club differs from a regular dinner party because it's immersive and interactive. Stand up and do a presentation to introduce your meal. Do research in advance on the internet to explain your theme and menu; reveal the provenance of your ingredients; work with your area of expertise and then share it.

Atmosphere is essential. This is your chance to launch the one-night-only restaurant of your dreams. Really make an effort: dress the table with candles and flowers and set the scene with lighting and music. The more effort you put in, the more you'll get out.

Collect cash for charity. Set aside a box where guests can deposit what they think the meal should cost. Count this up at the end of the night and donate your collection to the good cause of your choice.

End with a flourish. Send your guests home on a high. For example, glasses of fino sherry and homemade biscotti might be simple but they inject enduring wow factor.

PLAYLIST

We try to keep the atmosphere at Shells pretty chilled and mellow. But we have to love the music we play too. There's nothing worse than working eight hours with a really nasty soundtrack in the background. We change it regularly and also do playlists for different events. Some of the stuff we love at home is just too slow for Shells. Our speakers are beside the coffee machine, so during that morning caffeine rush the music helps us keep the pace up!

Our 10 ten artists that feature in Shells are:

- *Florence and the Machine*
- *Angus and Julia Stone* - chilled and calm with amazing lyrics
- *José Gonzalez*
- *Nouvelle Vague* - very mellow covers that give a nice lift
- *Pete Yorn and Scarlett Johansson* - they do a great duet that's pretty raw and has a cool beat
- *Lana Del Ray* - totally addictive
- *De La Soul* - creeps in there for Myles
- *Pistol Dreams* - a lovely surfy sound, our fave track is 'The Tallest Man on Earth'
- *Rhianna* - pops in there too with cool tunes for the weekend
- *Irish artists* - of course we have our fave local and Irish artists, from Damien Rice to local band Tucan and Kathy Jordan

THE HANGOVER

We've all been there. But some of us seem to bounce back better than others. Here are our tried-and-tested tips for a speedy recovery.

- Bacon – and lots of it! Don't do the fried eggs. It might seem like a good idea at first but I bet you won't eat them.
- Potato fries and a can of fizz – Chips are perfectly greasy and the soda is sugary and effervescent, even better if caffeinated.
- Tomato juice cocktail – Add extra Tabasco, celery salt and Worcestershire sauce. Make it, down it… and go back to bed!
- Cold pizza, cold glass of milk – Best served on the couch in your underwear and with sleep in your eyes! First thing in the morning while watching cartoons with the mute button on.

HANGOVER CURES

"Smoothies – something with vitamins in it. Or better yet, a Bloody Mary!"
Conor Heffernan, technology officer and customer

"Surf is a great hangover cure. It's so cold you can't think of anything else, and it wakes you up."
Sarah Heath, set designer and Shells waitress

"Alcohol is acidic, so to recover you need to alkalize your blood quickly with a seaweed bath or a smoothie of seaweed and green veg. It works – we prove it Sunday after Sunday after Sunday."
Neil Walton, Voya Seaweed Baths

"It's supposed to be the worst thing to do, but I normally depend on coffee. It takes a cup before I can even talk to anybody."
Fergus McCaffery, forestry consultant and customer

"Sleep! Then coffee, coffee, coffee and lots of water. I can't do hangovers – I suffer too much."
Sinead McGoldrick, former Shells manager

"I make a devilishly good Bloody Mary. You have to combine it with a couple of Nurofen Plus. Once you get one of those down you, so much the better."

Fred Symmons, forager and environmental consultant

"I really like the egg and soldiers in Shells! And Lucozade Orange sometimes."
Siobhan McGriskin, teacher and kayaker

"Fried eggs, beans and brown bread sorts me out."
Colly Moran, graphic designer and customer

"Don't stop drinking is my hangover cure. But I'm a publican – I have to say that don't I?"
Tricky Caheny, publican

"A good can of coke and a nice piece of cake – anything with sugar!"
Aoife McGowan

Grilled Cheese Sandwich

This is a simple dish, but the key is not scrimping on the cheese and using a good quality cheddar. You want the cheese to ooze out. It may be messy, but the clean up is worth it. A real hangover treat!

2 slices of thick cut bread, preferably homemade (don't use thin slices, it just won't work).

4 generous slices of vintage cheddar cheese

Butter

2 dollops of red onion marmalade (page 88)

- Heavily butter the outside of the bread.
- Build the sandwich with the cheddar and red onion marmalade.
- Preheat a steak griddle pan or a pan with a thick base until it's nice and hot. You don't need to use oil as the butter on the outside of the bread will prevent sticking.
- Once the pan is hot place the sandwich in. Leave for about two or three minutes and then flip it with a spatula. You want it to be golden on both sides.
- This is also amazing done on the barbecue. Just put it straight on the grill for a lovely smoky flavour. This comes with a warning though... it's addictive!

the bit at the back

LISTINGS

If you are visiting this beautiful area, here's some information on places to stay, where to eat, what pubs to go to and interesting activities. This corner of Ireland will enchant you so come and visit soon and set your spirit free!

ACCOMMODATION

Clarion Hotel Sligo

Located on the outskirts of Sligo town and overlooked by the majestic Benbulben Mountain is the four-star Clarion Hotel Sligo, which dates back to 1848 and designed by William Dean Butler. Facilities include; 162 bedrooms including 89 suites, Sinergie Restaurant, Kudos Bar & Restaurant, SanoVitae Health & Leisure Club, Essence Spa, two converted churches on site.
ADDRESS: Clarion Hotel, Clarion Road, Sligo
TEL: 071 911 9000
EMAIL: info@clarionhotelsligo.com
WEB: www.clarionhotelsligo.com

Cois Re Holiday Apartments

We offer 4 star Bord Failte approved luxury self catering accommodation in the heart of Yeats Country. These luxury self-catering holiday apartments are spacious and modern. Cois Ré is ideally situated for golf enthusiasts and surfers alike, being just a short walk to the beach and local golf course. We are also within easy walking distance of an array of bars, restaurants and other amenities.
ADDRESS: Cois Re Holiday Apartments, Strandhill, Co. Sligo.
TEL: 00353 (0) 87 9574358
EMAIL: carmel@coisreapartments.com
WEB: www.coisreapartments.com

Ocean Wave Lodge

Come and experience the warm welcome relaxed and easy going pace of life at the Ocean Wave Lodge in Strandhill, nestling at the foot of Knocknarea mountain and overlooking the sea. If you are after a family weekend, romantic getaway or even a week of surfing madness, then come and enjoy all that Strandhill has to offer. Bedrooms consist of family rooms, double and twin rooms, all at very competitive rates. All rooms are ensuite and linen and towels are provided .
ADDRESS: Top Road, Strandhill, Sligo
TEL: +353 (0)71 91 68115
EMAIL: info@oceanwavelodge.com
WEB: www.oceanwavelodge.com

Inishmulclohy Lodge Coney Island

Inishmulclohy Lodge is a three-star self catering lodge on Coney Island. Sleeps a maximum of six with all mod cons. Fantastic sea views two minutes from the beach, including Carty's Strand, a great surfing beach. Ideal for a traditional family holiday. Wards Pub is great for traditional music. Activities include surfing, deep sea fishing, boat trips, painting holidays. Wheelchair access.
TEL: 087 642 1482
EMAIL: eileenferguson5@gmail.com
WEB: www.nealgreig.com

Rosses Point Guesthouse

Rosses Point Guesthouse is a new and modern accommodation option in the heart of the beautifully scenic seaside village of Rosses Point, only five miles from Sligo town. A good value, fun alternative to the existing accommodation in the area.
ADDRESS: Rosses Point, Co. Sligo
TEL: +353 (0)86 351 2762
EMAIL: info@rossespointguesthouse.com
WEB: www.rossespointguesthouse.com

Seashore B&B

Seashore is an Award-Winning Country Home situated on a three-acre site, offering Luxury Accommodation. We are 8km from Strandhill and just 50 metres from the sea. Enjoy breakfast in the conservatory/diningroom overlooking Knocknarea, the Ox Mountains and Ballysadare Bay.
ADDRESS: Off Ballina Road, Lisduff, Ballysadare, Co.Sligo.
TEL/FAX: +353 (0) 7191 67827
MOBILE: +353 86 222 4842
EMAIL: seashore@oceanfree.net
WEB: www.seashoreguests.com

Temple House Estate

Temple House is a beautiful mansion where you can stay, enjoy a house party or hold your wedding.
ADDRESS: Ballinacarrow, Ballymote, Co. Sligo,
TEL: 00353 719183329
EMAIL: stay@templehouse.ie
WEB: www.templehouse.ie

Sligo Park Hotel and Leisure Club

Four-star hotel with 137 bedrooms. Bar carvery and bar menu available throughout the day. **Hazelwood Restaurant Dinner** – Sligo's favourite wedding venue. Plus Adventure Breaks from 124 euros per person. Join Sligo Park Health and Leisure Club for 3, 6 or 12 months.
ADDRESS: Sligo Park Hotel & Leisure Club, Pearse Road, Sligo.
TEL: +353 71 919 0400
FAX: +353 71 916 9556
EMAIL: sligo@leehotels.com
WEB: www.sligoparkhotel.com

The Guest Wing at Primrose Grange House

Full of character and charm and nestled on Knocknarea, Primrose Grange House is a beautiful listed Georgian Building with spectacular sea views. Tastefully refurbished providing a well-equipped, cosy getaway with sheltered garden & BBQ area. Close to the amenities Strandhill and Sligo offer – perfect for those searching for a unique hideout.
ADDRESS: Knocknarea, Sligo
TEL: 00353 876141639
EMAIL: primrosegrange@gmail.com
WEB: www.luxuryselfcateringsligo.com

The Strandhill Lodge and Suites

The Strandhill Lodge and Suites is a four-star Luxury guesthouse which sits in the picturesque seaside village of Strandhill, Co Sligo. Nestled in the shadow of Mount Knocknarea, this 21 room guesthouse, comprising 18 deluxe rooms and three Suites, with a mix of rooms with balconies, patios and superior two-room suites. Located 2 mins from Shells Café, Strandhill
ADDRESS: Strandhill Lodge and Suites, Top Road, Strandhill, Co Sligo
TEL: (353)71 9122122
EMAIL: info@strandhilllodgeandsuites.com
WEB: strandhilllodgeandsuites.com

Accommodation cont'd
Tawnylust Lodge & Leitrim Landscapes Guided Walks
Offer eco-friendly accommodation and fabulous walks 'off the beaten track'. Forage for wild herbs, mushrooms and unusual edibles. Hear the culinary history of our ancestors, get recipes and cooking tips.

ADDRESS: Manorhamilton, Ireland
TEL: 00353 719820083
EMAIL: info@tawnylustlodge.com
WEB: www. tawnylustlodge.com

EATING OUT
Cosgroves Deli
A treasure trove of deli goodies. Everything from fresh organic fruits to that hard to find herb. A great selection of olives, meats and Irish cheeses too.

ADDRESS: 32 Market Street, Sligo
TEL: 071 9142809

Kates Kitchen
Independent fine foods & toiletry store with delicious homemade lunches and treats to takeaway. Open Monday to Saturday. Do call!

ADDRESS: Kates Kitchen, 3 Castle Street, Sligo.
TEL: 071 91 43022
EMAIL: info@kateskitchen.ie
WEB: www.kateskitchen.ie

Sheerins Meatin Place Ballymote
Fifth Generation Butcher Adrian Sheerin, has been open in Ballymote for the last five years after taking over the family business. All our meat, poultry and vegetables are locally sourced and of the highest quality, customer service is our priority.

ADDRESS: Teeling Street, Ballymote
TEL: 719183671

Tra Ban Restaurant
Located in Strandhill above the Strand Bar, Tra Bhán Restaurant is rapidly establishing itself as a must-stop culinary destination of the North West. Specialising in fresh, local produce, Tra Bhán's mouth watering menu comprises of meat, seafood and vegetarian options.

ADDRESS: Above The 'Strand Bar', Strandhill, Sligo
TEL: (00353)719128402
EMAIL: trabanstrandhill@gmail.com

The Venue
The Venue is a Steak and Seafood Restaurant in Strandhill. "The food is marvelous, the view spectacular: a dining experience not to be missed and not soon forgotten." – *MyGuideIreland.com*

ADDRESS: The Venue, Bar & Restaurant, Strandhill, Sligo
TEL: (+353) 719168167
EMAIL: info@venuestrandhill.ie
WEB: www.venuestrandhill.ie

Maple Moose
Maple Moose is an authentic ice cream parlour in Strandhill. So get to Maple Moose and spoil yourself with crepes, waffles, whipped ice cream and check out our famous cold slab scoop ice cream mixes.

ADDRESS: Maple Mousse, Shore Road, Strandhill
TEL: 353 917168140
MOB: 353 872886915
EMAIL: byrneent@gmail.com

Source Sligo
A Restaurant, a Wine Bar and a Cookery School split over three levels in a landmark building on John Street, Sligo, Source is everything food and wine should be.

ADDRESS: 1 & 2 John Street, Sligo, Ireland Restaurant - Wine Bar - Cookery School
TEL: 0035371 9147605
EMAIL: info@sourcesligo.ie
WEBSITE: www.sourcesligo.ie

PUBS AND NIGHTCLUBS
The Harp Tavern
There's always a warm welcome at this renowned Sligo pub. Famous music venue with Trad Sessions every Monday night and lunchtime jazz every Sunday. 1pm onwards there's live music at the weekends. Parking and taxi rank adjacent - a visit is a must.

ADDRESS: The Harp Tavern, Quay Street, Sligo
TEL: 0719142473
EMAIL: sean@theharptavernsligo.com
WEB: www.theharptavernsligo.com

The Dunes tavern
The Dunes tavern is one of Strandhill's best bars. We offer a welcoming, friendly bar, picturesque beer garden with fantastic views of Knocknarae

mountain, games room and budget accommodation. We regularly host live music and our open mic is always a great night every Monday.

ADDRESS: Dunes Tavern, Top Road, Strandhill.
TEL: 0719168131
WEB: www.accommodationstrandhill.com

The Strand Bar
The Strand Bar is run by three former Irish surf team members famous for its live music and good food.

ADDRESS: The Strand Bar & Restaurant, Shore Road, Strandhill
TEL: 353 917168140
MOB: 353 872886915
WEB: www.thestrandbar.com
facebook.com/thestrandbar
twitter.com/thestrandbar

Velvet Room Nightclub
Opens Saturdays and Bank Holiday Sundays from 11.30pm til Late. Over 21s only.

ADDRESS: Velvet Room, Kempton Promenade, Sligo Town
Tel: Table Reservations - 00 353 71 9144721
EMAIL: info@velvetroom.ie
WEB: www.velvetroom.ie

ACTIVITY CENTERS
LSD Kiteboading
LSD Kiteboarding has a long standing reputation as one of the best kitesurfing schools in Ireland offering professional tuition and equipment sales. We provide a safe, fun and progressive learning experience as we introduce you to the sport of Kitesurfing.

ADDRESS: The Beach, Rosses Point, Co. Sligo
TEL: +353 (0) 86 805 1390
EMAIL: info@LSDKiteboarding.com
WEB: www.LSDKiteboarding.com

Strandhill Surf School
Strandhill Surf School is the centre of surfing in Strandhill, Sligo. We have a great location in a corner premises on the beachfront. Run by owner Paul Buchanan,from New Zealand, it is a great place to learn to surf or improve your surfing skills.

ADDRESS: Beach Front, Strandhill, Sligo, Ireland
MOBILE: + 353 (0) 87 2870817
TEL: + 353 (0) 71 9168483
EMAIL: strandhillsurfschool@gmail.com
WEB: www.strandhillsurfschool.com

Perfect Day Surf School

Established in 1998 – the original and best. Perfect Day surf school offers small group, family and individual lessons. 1-to-5 instructor to surfer ratio. Now offering Stand up Paddle lessons and tours.

ADDRESS: Elisha Hickey, Perfect Day Surf School, Shore Road, Strandhill, Co.Sligo
TEL: 0872897462 / 0872029399
EMAIL: info@perfectdaysurfing.ie
WEB: www.perfectdaysurfing.ie
www.standuppaddlessligo.ie

Northwest Adventure Tours

Specialising in on- and off-road guided biking and hiking tours in the stunning Northwest of Ireland. We are based in Sligo and operate all over the Northwest. We also offer full and half day trips, package holidays, bike hire and more. Check out our website for more details.

TEL: 0860229952
EMAIL: northwestadventuretours@gmail.com
WEB: www.northwestadventuretours.ie
You can also find us on Facebook and Twitter

ATTRACTIONS
Ewings Sea Angling and Boat Charters

Services available include general deep sea/shark angling, mackerel trips, Coney, Inishmurray Island water taxis, eco-tourism/sightseeing trips and catch 'n cook cruises. Rods and tackle for hire. Beginners welcome!

ADDRESS: Rosses Point, Co Sligo.
TEL: +353 (0) 868913618
EMAIL: info@sligoboatcharters.com
WEB: www.sligoboatcharters.com
FACEBOOK: www.facebook.com/SligoBoatCharters

The Sligo Traditional Singers

The Sligo Traditional Singers' Circle was set up to foster the art of Traditional and Sean Nós singing in Sligo. We hold a singing session at 10 pm on the second wednesday of each month in Durkin's Pub, Ballinacarrow. All singers and listeners most welcome
WEB: www.sligotradsingers.ie

The Roundabout Gallery

A must-see vast contemporary Art & Craft gallery. 100% of our stock is created by regional artisans. Quality, originality and a welcome

are guaranteed. We are open Monday – Saturday 10am – 6pm and Sunday 12pm - 6pm

ADDRESS: Collooney Roundabout, Collooney, Co. Sligo
TEL: 071 9118712
EMAIL: theroundaboutgallery@gmail.com
WEB: www.theroundaboutgallery.com

Waxon Surfboards

Ireland's design and shape custom surfboards. Conor and the Waxon team work with you to design, shape and create a surfboard to your individual specifications.

ADDRESS: Waxon Surfboards, Benbulben Craft Centre, Rathcormac, Sligo
TEL: 086 8212418
EMAIL: waxonsurfboards@ireland.com
Website: www.waxonsurfboards.ie

LimeGreen Umbrella

LimeGreen Umbrella is a Creative Collective of Artists & Makers from the Northwest of Ireland. Jewellery, paintings, green-wood furniture, drawings, ceramics, quilts, chopping boards, hand-carved spoons, handmade soap & handmade cards.
Monday-Saturday 9 - 6

ADDRESS: Lyons, Sligo town
TEL: (087) 6970064
EMAIL: limegreenumbrella@gmail.com
WEB: www.limegreenumbrella.wordpress.com

EVENTS & FESTIVALS

We love local events in Ireland. It's a great excuse for getting dressed up, running into friends and listening to music, with the promise of good drinks and superb food too. Here's a roundup of our faves.

March

Saint Patrick's Day Parade
A small, low-key celebration that doesn't take itself too seriously. All the pubs put on traditional music and there's a real party feel.
- Sligo Town, noon on 17 March

April

Feis Shligigh
A feis is a Gaelic arts and culture festival to promote tradition and pride. This one includes competitions in Irish dancing, classical music, English verse speaking, traditional music, drama and Irish language.
- Various locations, www.feis-shligigh.ie

May

Só Sligo Food Festival
During this showcase every restaurant makes a huge effort to put Sligo's food culture and rich local produce on the map. Enjoy free food and some great deals.
- Sligo Town, www.sosligo.com

June

Sea Sessions Surf Music Festival
A really relaxed, well-run festival that's easy to get to and easy to get around. Right on the beach, it attracts a young, cool crowd. They always have a big tent so it's virtually weatherproof too!
- Bundoran, www.seasessions.com

Culleenamore Races
There's a strong equestrian heritage in Ireland, but horse and pony racing on the beach isn't something you'll see every day. A really cool old tradition in the fresh seaside air.
- On the beach at Culleenamore

July

Sligo Jazz Project
An accessible, mellow event that's open to all ages. There's a good atmosphere, a real buzz and absolutely great music.
- Sligo Town, www.sligojazz.ie

Warrior of the Sea
A hardcore 6km open water swim. One the hardest things you'll ever see humans do; for extra points some tackle it in a swimsuit instead of a wetsuit!
- Rosses Point to Strandhill

Cairde Summer Festival
A really diverse festival encompassing all kinds of arts, with an itinerary starting in the morning and ending late every night. Great for seeing interesting stuff you'd never normally come across with plenty of cutting edge elements and free things too.
- Sligo Town, www.cairdefestival.com

Strandhill Show and Gymkhana
A nice community day out that involves all ages. Bigger and bigger each year, it's in the grounds of a big old home in a lovely position on the sea.
- Lisheen House Estate, www.strandhillshow.com

August

Warriors Run and Festival
A highlight - it's mental! The run itself is 15km, with the majority straight up and over Knocknarea. It's pretty intense with amazing scenery, lots of fancy dress and a limit of 800 competitors. All the pubs go mad in the evening with bands and dancing in the street.
- Strandhill, www.warriorsfestival.com

September

Culture Night Sligo
Taking place across Ireland, Culture Night is a free evening of entertainment, discovery and adventure. Arty, creative Sligo is one of the 30 participating cities.
- Sligo Town, www.culturenight.ie

October

Sligo Live
A lively, big weekend where nearly every venue takes part offering music from morning to night. Acts include traditional, roots, jazz, acoustic, folk – even hip-hop!
- Sligo Town, www.sligolive.ie

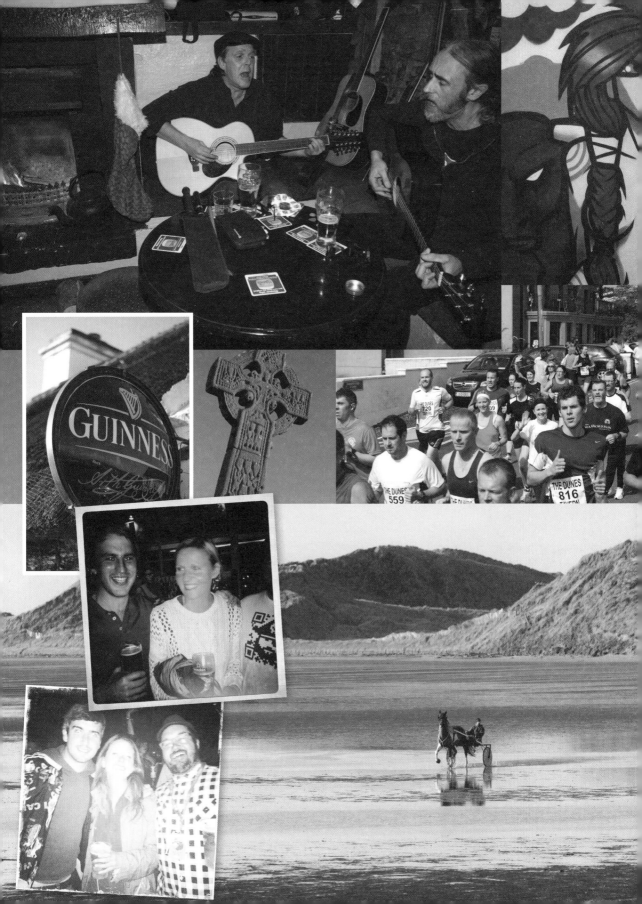

NOTES

USEFUL CONVERSION TABLES

OVEN TEMPERATURE CONVERSIONS

Farenheit	Centigrade	Gas Mark	Description
225 F	110 C	¼	Very Cool
250 F	130 C	½	
275 F	140 C	1	Cool
300 F	150 C	2	
325 F	170 C	3	Very Moderate
350 F	180 C	4	Moderate
375 F	190 C	5	
400 F	200 C	6	Moderately Hot
425 F	220 C	7	Hot
450 F	230 C	8	
475 F	240 C	9	Very Hot

US LIQUID MEASUREMENTS

1 gallon	4 quarts	3.79 L (can round to 4L)
1 quart	2 pints	.95 L (can round to 1L)
1 pint	2 cups	16 fl. oz. or 450 ml
1 cup	8 fl oz	225 ml (can round to 250ml)
1 tablespoon (Tbsp.)	½ fl oz	16 ml (can round to 15 ml)
1 teaspoon (tsp.)	⅓ tablespoon	5 ml

BRITISH LIQUID MEASUREMENTS

1 UK pint	5.6 ltrs	
1 UK liquid oz	0.96 US liquid oz	
1 pint	570 ml	16 fl oz
1 breakfast cup	10 fl oz	½ pint
1 tea cup	⅓ pint	
1 Tablespoon	15 ml	
1 dessert spoon	10 ml	
1 teaspoon	5 ml	⅓ Tablespoon
1 ounce	28.4 g	can round to 25 or 30
1 pound	454 g	
1 kg	2.2 pounds	

INTERNATIONAL LIQUID MEASUREMENTS

Country	Standard Cup	Standard Teaspoon	Standard Tablespoon
Canada	250 ml	5 ml	15 ml
Australia	250 ml	5 ml	20 ml
UK	250 ml	5 ml	15 ml
New Zealand	250 ml	5 ml	15 ml

NOTES

INDEX

THANKS!

Wow! What a journey both Shells and this book have been on. We never thought it would be so successful and fun, so first and foremost we want to thank our customers, for coming back every day and for encouraging us to be as good as we can. Our customers are a major source of inspiration for us and they really are the nicest ones you could hope for. So many are now friends!

Big thanks to both our families, for supporting us, for contributing to the look, feel, design and running of Shells and this amazing book. (Paula, Fergal and Shelley for their truly inspirational design and artwork, Susan and Sarah for the shoulders to lean on and for testing the recipes, Fuzzy – for not following the recipes! – and Phil for being 'the rock'.)

Special thanks to all our staff who have contributed to the book and kept Shells going while we wrote, tested and tasted the recipes. (Bernie for her dog, Knocknarae stories and laughter and everyone at Shells who gave us their input and support.)

A big warm thanks to Mike (photographer) and Shannon (writer) for intense, fun times pulling everything together, and also to Ocean Wave Lodge for hosting the crew during the duration of the book.

A special thanks to Louise and Dave for piecing everything together and having this amazing vision for the book – too cool for skool! Also to our neighbours Voya and Perfect Day Surf School, for their knowledge, support and locations.

To all our suppliers (Richard Woodmartin, Sheerins Meatin Place, Bluebell Falls) foragers (Fred), gardeners (Jessie), drinkers (Tricky and Shane) – all friends and foodies who have given up their time to share their passion with us and allow us to use their vast knowledge for this book…
Thank you guys!

And finally, to YOU, for buying this book and supporting local industry, local products and local food.

Bon appétit. Eat well!

Jane & Myles

Jane & Myles